A Standard Journey

5 horses, 2 people, and 1 tent

Jackie Parry

ISBN: 978-0-9875515-6-6

Though this is a work of nonfiction, I have changed some names to protect the identities of the people I've written about.

I have also provided a glossary at the back of this book.

Dedication

To our amazing boys

The Fab Five

> *Charlie Cullen – 'Charlie'*
> *Dreamers Fiasco – 'Neddy-boy'*
> *Psycho Stevie – 'Stevie'*
> *Yrubla – 'Spirit'*
> *Den's Passion – 'Dommie'*

CONTENTS

Ode to the Horse

Where in this wide world can man find nobility without pride,
friendship without envy or beauty without vanity?

Here, where grace is laced with muscle and strength by gentleness
confined.

He serves without servility; he has fought without enmity.

There is nothing so powerful, nothing less violent,
There is nothing so quick, nothing more patient.

England's past has been borne on his back; all our history is his
industry.
We are his heirs; he, our inheritance.

The Horse!

'Ode to the Horse' by Ronald Duncan

Reproduced by kind permission from the managing director of the
Horse of the Year Show (HOYS).

This iconic poem was written by Ronald Duncan especially for the
HOYS in 1954, and has been read at the end of each show since
1955.

Introducing Our Boys (The Team)

Background: We adopted five horses from the Standardbred Performance and Pleasure Horse Association (SPPHA). Through injury or lack of winnings, many Standardbreds (or trotters) are retired and desperately need new homes.

Two of our boys had already been re-homed for a short period after retiring from racing and required re-adoption for different reasons. The rest came straight from racing yards.

Allow me to introduce our boys:

Charlie (Charles! when naughty)
Too big at 16hh, light bay, eight years old. Lanky and square in build, a little stubborn and cowardly. He has a head the size of a suitcase and the kindest eyes I have ever seen. He became my 'war-horse.'

Ned (Neddy-boy)
15hh, liver chestnut, nine years old. His nerves were shredded, and quite often his body was rigid with fear. He jumped at leaves blowing in the wind, but my goodness did he change into the most willing, giving animal that I have ever witnessed. Ned's nicely put together, strong, proportionate to the eye, pretty head, but powerful and keen. Ned watches *everything*.

Stevie
15.2hh, dark bay, five years old. Nothing fazes Stevie, except cuddles. He's willing to trust in everything you ask of him and treat you gently, unless you use too many leg-aids. As time goes on, love becomes part of his repertoire too, as well as patience with his family. His powerful legs and bouncy trot carry his firm body and teddy-bear look.

Spirit

15.2hh, bay, nine years old. Our *cool-dude* has definitive boundaries and can be moody. Spirit should wear shades! He works hard, plays hard, and embarks on cheeky fun. He became all muscle, a solid work-horse, but a horse who knows himself completely, including what he wants and when he wants it! Intelligent to the point where he knows when to show gratitude, and how to train Noel and me!

Dom (Dommie)

15.1hh, dark bay, four years old. Young, playful. Life's one big game; he's slim – almost dainty – but strong and beautiful. Dom brings joy and fun into the troop but will do whatever it is you ask of him. He loves all the horses and Noel and me with equal measure – as long as he can roll in water, mud, and sand at will!

There are photos of the boys in the centre of this book. For the full photo album and the BNT map please visit:
http://jackieparry.com/photo-album/

1

We Won't Even Have A Sink!

Galloping down the mountain to find a gun to shoot one of our horses, I realised that I had bitten off more than I could chew.

My borrowed horse sensed my fear as we plunged down the trail. My mind focused on the gun, a necessity to terminate excruciating pain. There was a broken horse on the ridge. He had released a knowing groan as his fetlock snapped.

Plunge, jump, ford – I squeezed my aching legs around my brave mount. We both expelled urgent breaths from our flared nostrils. *I had to find a gun!*

Sweat and tears mingled, running clean streaks along my grubby face, my eyes stinging. My heart banged in my chest, while the horse's heart thrummed beneath my calf muscles. Time slowed as if we hurtled through syrup.

I cursed Noel - it was his idea. Not to shoot the horse, but living with horses twenty-four seven while trekking along the Bicentennial National Trail (BNT). We had rescued five lost beasts that could have been destined for dog meat. Over many months of struggle, we had transformed the seven of us into a team.

There's a thrill to exploring remote locations in Australia by horseback that you can't reach by car. The added challenge of carrying all you need, plus the inherent joy of riding, all culminated into a new adventure.

We'd planned to spend at least two years working in NSW after our previous escapades sailing around the world in a ten-metre boat. After selling that boat and a two year stint of earning money, we had purchased another boat in San Francisco and spent two years traversing the southern Pacific Ocean and sailing back to Australia, ultimately sailing around the world one and a half times.

While sailing, and particularly when bouncing around in lumpy seas, we'd often dreamed about a land-based journey encompassing the same freedom sailing offers. Ideas of riding horses along trails that were void of people and cars floated into our thoughts and discussions, but we didn't think it was possible. Once we learned about the trail, though, we saw the possibilities.

Noel and I are kindred spirits. We crave freedom, movement, and the adrenaline rush of a challenge. Away from people, houses, offices, roads, and cars, I find an inner sense of peace and contentment: my headspace changes; I can breathe. Not from lack of pollution but from being without the constraints and restrictions of life.

It started young for me, my desire to be carefree. At fourteen I'd argued with my dad and yelled, 'I just want to be free!' I was mortified when he told me no one is ever free. But I've learned that I can get close, very close. It's taken me a long time, but now I understand who I am.

It was February 2013, and our inner travel-devil told us it was time to sell everything – again – and become vagrants – again. We'd learned that travel and land-based responsibilities don't mix – the freedom is marred.

So, we had learned about the trail. We'd found the way to bring a dream to life. We made up our minds; we became blinkered.

The Bicentennial National Trail is Australia's long distance, multi-use recreational trekking route, stretching 5,330 kilometres from Cooktown in tropical far north Queensland to Healesville in Victoria. The trail follows the foothills of the Great Dividing Range and the Eastern Escarpment.

We sold everything and put our small cottage in NSW on the market. We reverted back to the 'good ol' days' of our first years of marriage, and lived with the bare minimum.

The mindset of selling up was easy; physically it was hard work, but mentally it wasn't a big deal. We'd done it before and had learned that inanimate objects don't give you a better life, buy you more time, or make you happy. *Now* is important, not things; each minute, every moment, connections, the sky, emotions, laughter.

Our good friends, Clive and Andrea, own a spare cottage (as you do on six-hundred glorious acres in Kangaroo Valley, NSW). We planned to rent the small home and keep our horses there too. We just needed the horses! The decision to take on horses wasn't hard by any means; they were my first love. The connection I feel with these creatures is overpowering. I am not socially inept, but I am incredibly sensitive, and I do analyse what people may or may not think of me on a regular basis – horses don't judge me by what I say. They don't worry if I make a bad joke, or if I fumble while relaying a story. They won't roll their eyes when I can't recall which president or king was reigning in whatever year. I can relate to horses all the time.

We'd been back on land for a year after sailing, softening physically and mentally. Spongy feet, protected by shoes day-in, day-out, would need toughening. The cushions that caressed our buttocks and the car that provided instant transport would be replaced by firm saddles.

When we revealed our plans to Noel's daughter, Mel, and his brother, Colin, they both looked at us a bit strangely, and Col asked, 'Have you sat on a horse recently?'

Noel pondered for a while. 'Erm, the last time was forty years ago, but I did lead one by the head collar the other day.' We all went a bit quiet.

Colin weaved his fingers together and turned to me. 'Well,' he said, 'at least *you* have lots of experience with horses.' We all felt a bit better, until I calculated that my last foray with the horsey world was over twenty years ago!

With that revelation, we all broke into nervous laughter. We sipped our tea and avoided eye contact, all picturing real and imagined horrors.

'There'll be some giggles along the way,' I said to Colin.

'Keep the camera on Noel,' he advised. Little did I know, it would be me the camera should be turned to.

While the decision to take on this challenge may seem like a whim, I can say that it definitely was – in one way. It's something we'd thought about, and we'd found a way to do it. That's just like Noel and me – it's there, so why not do it? But now, I can't help wondering if the decision was made seventeen years ago. I'd met Noel then, and at that time my life felt like it had skidded to an abrupt halt and then flown off in another direction while I hung on to the tails! Back then, in the UK, I'd recently lost the first man I was going to marry. Leukaemia had claimed him. My heart was in a million pieces, and I had run away to Australia and found Noel; he helped me put myself back together and take my life back under control. So, perhaps the culmination of losing someone, then meeting Noel so quickly, losing my way, then finding my way, maybe *that* was the start of the journey. The recipe of two ordinary people coming together with remarkable imaginations and wills: two people joining with a smattering of malcontent, and a desire to find contentment and wring out every experience from each moment. To define these emotions now requires more effort than the actual decision to go at the time. Neither of us went through the mental agony of 'the why' – we knew it was possible, we liked the idea, so quite simply we did it.

Or was it because travel had become a habit? Running away from a painful past set me on the travelling road, and I hadn't stopped for seventeen years; it wasn't just travel anymore; it was a way of life, freedom, space, headspace...

The one thing I do know is that to be constantly challenged is a craving that is deeply woven into the fabric of my being. Not just great undertakings such as trekking with five horses, but day-to-day too – anything from renovating to writing to new languages. If it isn't tough, I become bored; if life is wishy-washy, I'll actively seek something to test my resolve and push my limits. I don't have a desire to prove to others, just myself; I must quench that thirst for achievement. Doing extraordinary things creates bonds between you and those who are with you, and that creates addictive emotions – for me, it will happen time and again.

A few weeks later as the vivid and erratic thoughts of what we were planning plagued my mind, a few home truths struck me.

'We won't even have a sink!' I said, clutching the metal sides of our kitchen basin lovingly. But Noel wasn't worried.

'That's okay, we'll use a billabong!' My bearded bush-husband raised his twinkling eyes to mine in challenge.

The daunting array of necessary equipment stretched the list to impossible lengths: tent, sleeping bags, buckets, panniers, saddles, ropes, halters, hats...

'The horses come first,' I said to Noel, as he straddled a chair while searching through tent catalogues; I still couldn't help but glance at my sink and the hot water tap that I knew I'd miss.

'What? Can't we just put them on the stand and turn the ignition off, like a motorbike?' he said, wearing his silly grin. 'I was wondering how you're going to manage pitching the tent in the rain alone.' He rubbed his hands together as if he'd figured it all out.

'What are you most concerned about?' I asked.

'My bottom!' Noel's derriere is wee, with no padding at all. Even with my well-protected bottom, I knew I would suffer.

'We'll have to work up to it, a little each day; before we know it, we'll be fine – it'll be like becoming familiar with moving around on the boat.' Cajoling our hips, knees, and ankles into foreign positions would create another set of challenges too.

As our thoughts ebbed and flowed, we started to discuss toilet paper. *How much do we use a week? Will we need more if one of us has an upset stomach?*

'We'll need less if we eat less meat, which we will,' Noel said. I wondered how many other couples discussed the amount of toilet paper they needed on a day-to-day basis.

I also had to think about sanitary products for my monthly period. I couldn't bury purchased sanitary products; they are chemically treated, and animals would dig them up, upsetting the landowners and causing untold potential problems. Let's not dwell on that too much. These products are burnable, but with the Australian weather, open fires were going to be few and far between. Aside from the logistical thoughts, I was also trying to avoid treated products for health reasons. So I researched 'how to make sanitary pads,' and, as usual, Google spat out a heap of ideas and advice from people who thought of doing this eons ago! I found the simplest instructions, printed them out, and then hoped I hadn't already sold the sewing kit! The instructions included the right material for absorption and how to wash them out. This seemed the simplest solution. No chemicals, no waste, and only a bush or back-of-saddle needed for a drying platform. There were lots of different ideas; one was to safety-pin the material in place. I quickly dismissed this approach, the thought of sitting on a horse with a pin near my privates was enough to make me squirm.

Even with the peculiarity of bathroom discussions and the effort of selling everything we owned, I breathed a sigh of relief that

I had found Noel. We have such similar thoughts and desires, and whenever one of us has an idea, it isn't long before the other is on board. Our agreed philosophy on tackling adventures was total immersion – it was all or nothing; we'd 'packed up' our lives several times to vanish into the oceans, other lands, and now, the bush.

As with all new escapades, we met new people. We made friends on social media. I started to follow an adventurous woman who was traversing the trail alone with three horses. I also began chatting to Sue, from NSW, who was hoping to tackle the trail with her friend Lynne, in Queensland. We swapped information, stories, worries, and excitement and decided to meet up at a pack-saddle workshop in April.

Noel, Sue, and I became instant friends, and later, when we met her husband, Bill, he quickly joined in the camaraderie. We were learning together and sharing different pockets of expertise.

'Don't buy expensive saddle blankets,' Sue advised. 'Buy a woollen blanket from the charity shop and cut that to shape.' This was excellent advice as we wanted breathable material next to the horses' skin.

Weight was a huge factor. Whilst researching camping equipment, Noel became terribly excited when he found a lighter tent.

'That's one hundred and twenty grams lighter; we can take another jar of Vegemite if we buy this tent!' Packing was going to be an interesting exercise. Noel was becoming a camping gear expert; I knew I'd be in charge of making it all fit. I am the master at packing up houses and stowing gear on a small boat. As a young woman, I moved through many relationships and a lot of homes, and I've had a lot of practice.

We booked into the pack-saddle workshop – the itinerary sounded perfect for beginners like us. We continued to note people's reactions with amusement. Good friends were supportive, some people admired what we were taking on, and others clearly felt sorry for us – which was understandable.

You have to be brave to take on different voyages. I am not talking about the physical and mental ability. I mean opting out of what's considered 'normal.' Some people think we are brave to be able to let everything go and follow our hearts. Others feel sorry for us, as we have a level of malcontent that drives us to new endeavours. For me, it is just about escape and freedom. It makes me feel ill to work in an office; that's why I haven't done it for years – I just can't. Boxed in, fake lighting, flickering screens, and my bid for freedom becomes chronic. When I drive along roads and peer at the rows and rows of houses with square gardens, my breath shortens and my lungs won't fill, as if they are being squeezed. As far as we know, we have one shot at this life, and I am poised with my sprinting shoes on!

2

Blind Panic

Sarah and Ralph, the pack-saddle workshop organisers, took us under their wing. They couldn't believe that people so naive would contemplate pack-saddling, full time! When asked about our horses, we received worried glances when we admitted we hadn't got any yet. At the workshop, we were keen to develop contacts to help us search for horses. I was fearful of buying a *ringer*, a horse that had been drugged for the viewing.

As the pack-saddle weekend progressed, it was difficult to find quality time with the experienced trail-goers as there was so much going on. However, we discussed our horse-purchase worries with Ralph, and he mentioned the Standardbred Association.

'They rescue trotters who are still young but too old to trot, or have been retired due to an injury, or are no longer winning,' he explained. 'Most of these horses have many good years left but go for dog meat, as there are just too many of them.'

The Standardbred Pleasure and Performance Horse Association (SPPHA) runs an adoption programme to help save lives. We had looked at their website previously and thought about making contact. But we didn't fit into their criteria. Ralph encouraged us to look again. I contacted the association when we arrived back home and laid out our story and ideas. They, too, took us under their wing and set to work, finding us suitable animals.

We were happy to be able to help save some horses and promote their organisation along the way. The monetary savings on not having to buy animals was certainly welcomed, especially when we delved further into all the gear we'd need, to say nothing of the ongoing costs of care and food for our team. I was thrilled to be able to provide horses with a second chance; it fitted right in to my ethos on life – the 'ordinary' taking on the 'extraordinary.' I wouldn't feel the impact of these thoughts until much later, though, and in ways different from what I imagined. There were additional struggles, but also preciousness beyond logic.

There was a compromise, too. Most of these animals were broken to harness, not to saddle. So to add to the fun of the enterprise, it was up to me to break these animals in. Riding again in my forties was quite different from in my twenties; for a start, everything hurt so much more, although the pain did create quite an incentive to stay on board.

After the pack-saddle workshop and endless research and reading, our heads were at bursting point. In June we moved to Kangaroo Valley, although we hadn't sold our house in Greenwell Point. As a result, we were frustratingly spread over two houses. But all of a sudden we had four horses – and I was in heaven!

Spirit was the first horse home. He'd actually been rescued a few months before, but his current owner could no longer keep him.

'Be warned, he'll test you out,' she stated gravely. Even looking at his photo, I could tell he was Spirit in name and nature.

After arranging the pick-up date, I could hardly sit still waiting until we could collect him. We had by now purchased a car that could handle pulling a trailer (float). We hired a trailer, and with humming excitement that was barely contained, we drove to collect the first of our new family.

I had purchased a head collar, lead rope, hay net, and travellers for Spirit. The travellers would wrap around his lower legs to protect him while in the float. I had to laugh when Noel placed these over his own knees while driving, before the car warmed up.

Spirit called to us when we stepped out of our car. He was well looked after, but lonely. Horses are herd animals; they need the company of other horses. He trotted over and gratefully accepted a carrot. He was wary; we'd been told that local drunks had been harassing him at night. I was desperate to transport him to somewhere safe. His current owner was kind, and we all agreed that her friend would load Spirit into the trailer. The rest of us were too emotional; Spirit needed someone calm. We all assumed that as he'd previously travelled in a horse-lorry, he'd be okay in a trailer. With hesitation, he trustingly stepped in.

I decided to stand with him in the trailer until we hit the highway, just a few minutes down the road. I noticed, too late and with a small amount of alarm, that the jockey door couldn't be opened from the inside. The plan was to keep a mobile phone with me so I could ring Noel if I had a problem. Noel slowly eased the car into gear and smoothly pulled away, and Spirit panicked. A wave of terror clutched my stomach as I patted my pockets; I'd left my phone in the car.

The whites of his eyes were a silent scream; he hopped from one foot to another as he tiptoed along the line towards blind panic. I peered out the back of the trailer and studied my surroundings; the metal partition was just a bar. I was trapped with a frightened, half-tonne beast. *I'm not going to get out of here alive,* I thought.

I cooed, stroked, and offered carrots, but Spirit was in his own personal hell. He stomped, snorted, and sweated. I banged on the small window at the front to try to alert Noel. I was bordering on panic myself.

The next moment, we jerked to a halt. Noel opened the jockey door, and I fell out.

'Oh, thank goodness,' I said. 'Did you hear me knocking on the window?'

'No, I heard some stomping and noticed I still had your phone.'

'I couldn't get out, he was starting to panic,' I said breathlessly. 'He'll have to figure it out on his own!'

Riding in the float was one of the dumbest decisions I have ever made, and I was lucky Noel stopped the car. It's actually illegal to travel with a horse like that. If Spirit had truly panicked, I wouldn't have stood a chance.

The smooth drive along the highway calmed Spirit, and he munched his hay. When we reached home, he carefully backed out down the ramp, searched the new surroundings, and let go of an enormous snort. He stood on his toes, danced, snorted more, and frolicked. *How am I going to handle him?* I thought, trying to hide my doubts from Noel.

At Kangaroo Valley, Andrea also kept her two boys, Jet and Cedar. These lucky horses roamed around one hundred acres, and we hadn't seen them for a couple of days. We led Spirit into Jet and Cedar's paddock, showing him as much of the perimeter as we could. There were cows nearby for company, and he relaxed while pulling at short grass. He had no idea he had horse-company. We took him for a walk to the adjoining paddock, where he was free to wander. He followed us for a while but soon turned tail, back to the cows.

The next day, we strolled into the paddock. It was foggy. Spirit accepted an apple and then just disappeared into the fog, and we left to run some errands. We returned that afternoon, and the three horses were standing at the gate together as if to show off. I swear they all had big grins plastered across their faces. Jet and Cedar welcomed Spirit with open hooves. I could almost hear Spirit say, *Look what I found!*

Spirit was both handsome and pretty and knew it – not in a tarty way, but in a soft, playful way. He loved attention – just craved it. You could almost hear him say, *Touch me anywhere, just touch me!* Spirit started in high spirits. Our first walk was complete with snorts and jumps. If he could have, he would have said: *You've let me make friends; let me go play!* He couldn't believe his luck: hundreds of acres to roam, mates to play with, and two slaves who fed him carrots!

We were riding Spirit most days; sometimes he thought the narrow creek scarier than the day before – it was just his way of making sure we were alert – but most of the time he revelled in all the attention.

Two weeks later, Charlie and Ned arrived. Charlie was lanky, a touch gaunt, with a big Roman nose and the kindest, softest eyes I had ever seen. Ned, a pretty liver chestnut, was his mate.

Their previous owners dropped them off with the fleeting remarks, 'I don't *think* they'd hurt you' and 'You know, Charlie's never had a saddle on?'

We released them into the paddock and made introductions. Neddy bucked and kicked with excitement and fear. He stuck to Charlie like glue. They kept looking around in disbelief, as if amazed that they had *all this grass* to eat!

Charlie didn't like his ears being touched one bit. I love horse's ears, and if they become accustomed to this touch, a gently rubbed ear can be soothing for them. Just seven days later, he was allowing me to stroke his ears. I caught his eyes shutting with relaxation and pleasure as I gently tugged his big ears.

Ned and Charlie were nervous; within a week Charlie was a lot more settled. Ned was getting there but still a bit jumpy. I had faith that he'd calm.

That left just one more horse to complete our string of four.

'You're kidding?' said Noel. 'You want me to take on a horse called Psycho Stevie?' He placed his hands firmly on his hips as if to appear brave, but his head was shaking.

I grinned. I thought it was funny, but I too couldn't help being concerned; how had he earned his name?

Stevie walked onto the trailer like a lamb. But it had rained all day, and the creek crossing into the property had become too dangerous to traverse. We were just two tantalising kilometres from his new home, but we couldn't risk it. We had to park the vehicles and cross the creek on the suspended-walk bridge and slop our way home.

A neighbouring farmer kindly housed Stevie in his yard for a few days, with just a little Shetland for company next door, on a concrete yard. We drove down to see him several times a day, but he looked bewildered and lonely. Finally, after two days, the creek dropped and we attempted a crossing. I saddled him up, confident as he'd been ridden previously, and jumped on. He set off with a keen bound and excitement for his next adventure. Puddles lined the country road, and Stevie jumped or wormed his way around each and every one.

'Good grief, Stevie,' I said to him. 'How am I going to ride you through the creek?' The creek, when Noel and I had checked, was only about a foot deep, but running fast.

Noel had followed me partway in the car. 'If you drive back to the house and grab Spirit and meet me at the creek, seeing another horse on the other side might entice Stevie to cross.'

'Good idea,' Noel replied. 'I'll bring some carrots too.'

Stevie had a fabulous high-leg action, which literally threw me up out of the saddle when he trotted. It was great fun, and it made rising to the trot effortless. But, such was the 'bounce' with each lift that I climbed higher and higher, so much so that I had to rein him in and start again. I found I trotted with a big grin! Halfway back to his new home, Stevie stopped and refused to walk on, and I thought, *Uh oh*. But we had approached a dark part of the road where the trees stretched over the top, clutching together to make a shady canopy. With gentle persuasion and a firm voice, I convinced him to trust me and walk on through.

I reached the creek, and there was no sign of Noel. The neighbour's dog kept us company, ignoring my commands of, 'Go home, will ya!'

At the creek, Stevie stopped. I didn't ask him to go forward; instead I jumped off and gave him a good pat.

'You are such a good boy, trusting me and bringing me here safely.' We stood for a while and watched the dog run through the water. We were both glad to see another living thing make it through!

I stood by Stevie's head and started to walk confidently. Obediently, he kept in stride with me and didn't hesitate for a moment. The muddy water trickled over my feet, my toes curled with the coolness, and my boots overflowed, but I wasn't going to stop. Stevie received his first big hug when we reached the other side – and he didn't like it. I felt him tense, and he flicked one ear forward and one back, a sign of confusion. Slowly he tried to stretch his neck and head away from my embrace.

I wasn't sure if it was because of the life he had had, being a trotter, or just not knowing me. Stevie had come from a kind home previously (directly after racing), but he hadn't been there long. Maybe he had had little affection in his life or was just the aloof type.

I hopped back on Stevie, my soggy boots squelching. As we reached the property's gate, Noel appeared with Spirit. Both Spirit and Stevie looked at each other – heads high, ears alert, wide, happy eyes.

Noel also had his head high, his ears and eyes alert. 'I can't believe you got here that quick,' he said, pulling Spirit to a halt. 'How'd you do at the creek?'

'Like a dream. I lead him through; he didn't hesitate. I couldn't believe it after he hopped over all the little puddles.'

Noel and I grinned at each other, something we'd do a lot – amid the heartfelt tears that would follow.

Stevie settled in with the rest of the team and Andrea's two (Jet and Cedar). All of a sudden, there was a herd of horses, and I was the happiest girl alive.

Taekwondo Ninja Horses

The first time Noel attempted to catch Ned, he consistently catapulted his entire body five feet in the air, bucking too (Ned that is, not Noel).

'At that point,' Noel reminisced that evening, 'I should have closed the gate, climbed in the car, and kept driving.' This made me giggle, but it was Noel's next observation that provided severe stomach-cramping guffaws.

'I'm still trying to get over watching Ned scratch his ear with his hind hoof!' As Noel remembered this incredulous picture, his voice became taut. 'Obviously, there is not one safe place to stand near a horse. We should have full body armour! They're like little Taekwondo Ninjas, wiggling their toes near their ears for goodness sake!' It was my turn to snort. These 'horse happenings,' to me, were everyday life – I'd grown up with horses. To Noel they were a wonder, and to see it through his eyes was fascinating and highly amusing.

I was responsible for these four horses now, when growing up I hadn't born the entire brunt of that accountability. My parents had given up so much so we could have horses as kids (I have two older sisters; one adored horses too, the other could take them or leave them – albeit enjoying them immensely at times). My folks didn't travel, eat out often, or go on extravagant excursions; they did very little for themselves, but took great pleasure in watching their children enjoy their lives around animals. I'm both deeply grateful for the opportunities I was given and slightly in awe of how they coped. I was now being starkly exposed to the reality of the entire responsibility of owning horses.

As the days passed, we both noted that everything smelled of horse: our clothes, chairs, hair, and skin. I realised that the smell I loved so much had permeated into our food when Noel stated, 'I am eating a raisin, and it tastes exactly like hay!' His nose scrunched up in disgust.

These observations made the journey even better than I had imagined. Most days I would clutch my stomach and wipe tears of laughter from my grubby face.

First, we had to convince our team to trust us. Each day we worked together. I taught them how to lunge in a circle and listen to my voice. We backed Charlie (i.e. sat on him). He was quite startled to find I had disappeared from his side and appeared on his back. As I sat there quietly, he curved his scrawny neck around to look at me as if to say, 'What on earth are you doing up there?' But he didn't protest (even after several months of riding, once I'd hopped on board, he would still swing his enormous head around and look up at me on his back). Charlie learned to listen to my gentle leg and voice commands; soon I could keep my legs still and use only my voice. His body eased into suppleness, and although he always checked it was me on his back, he eventually lost the startled glare.

We had to be so gentle with Neddy-boy. He was frightened of everything. However, once he learned to trust us, he became braver and braver, a real trooper in fact. While sitting on board, I'd appreciate his sure-footed strides and eagerness. His body was less tense when we sat on him, as if he found comfort in having someone so close.

Noel and I rode Charlie and Ned. While we explored new terrain, they were reassured by being together. Noel gelled with Neddy and sat well in the saddle, even with Ned's quick step, and I adored Charlie's huge strides. Ned proved his sure-footedness. From one paddock to the next, we usually traversed a steep decline, then rode back up into the next paddock. The alternative was to cut across the sheer hill and pick a path through a tricky, narrow ravine. We planned to take the long route until we were all better acquainted. But Ned had different ideas. One day, he suddenly turned right and headed along the steep short-cut. Noel 'asked' him a few times to go down along the wider track, but Ned was set on where he was going. He was walking, but striding with determined intent.

'Okay, Ned, if that's the way you want it.' Noel said, and I watched, amused and impressed as Noel's little bottom balanced perfectly in the saddle.

Charlie watched too; he didn't have Ned's balance, not yet – he was still adjusting to a weight on his back. I was content to sit there; it was a long way down for me!

'I don't know about you, Charlie, but I think we ought to stick with safe and sure at the moment.'

Charlie provided his agreement by walking down the wider, muddy course along the safer route.

At the bottom, we both peered up to see Neddy almost on his side; the pair of them appeared to be lying down as the hill was so steep. But sure enough, Ned knew where to place his feet, and Noel had the wit and grace to just sit, stay balanced, and let Ned sort it out. It was incredible to watch. As Charlie and I paced around the corner and back up the hill, Ned and Noel rested together, puffing out the adrenaline and sharing a big grin!

'Well done, you!' I said. 'You have magnificent balance!'

'Ned made the decision. It was easy to just sit deeply in the saddle and relax; I enjoyed that.' Noel's wide smile said it all. I knew I could relax a bit more. Noel had far more ability than he admitted and an obvious natural talent.

We were starting to gather equipment, much of it from America, where pack-saddling is a big business. There were a few industrious individuals beginning to set up pack-saddling equipment in Australia, but they were expensive. Shipping equipment from America was cheaper! Plus the States had many additional items we needed. It was cost-effective, quicker, and easier to order it all from one place.

We are not rich; we make savings where we can, but already expenses were mounting. However, by comparison we'd be living cheaply. We had no rates, electric bills, water bills, no car to run, smart clothes to buy, expensive restaurants and entertainment to fund. We would rarely use our phones (lack of coverage and desire). Working is far more expensive than not – you just have to be smart by making adjustments to your lifestyle to suit your income and/or savings.

We buy our clothes from charity shops; we don't use credit cards (we don't have any). If we want something, we save up to purchase it; we have no loans. We are careful with food and the amount of hot water we use – we do not take shorter or colder showers, but we'll turn the shower off while soaping up. This may appear ridiculous, but *every* little bit helps. I cut Noel's hair and have become adept at cutting mine. Taking care of every dollar means every dollar takes care of us.

The smartest thing we've done is to turn our lives into the entertainment. I sometimes experience big waves of contentedness; it's such fun being me!

As the small cottage started to fill with the heady scent of leather, our walking space diminished. Thick saddle blankets, leather straps, padded saddles, and ropes filled the floor. I left much of the saddle decision-making to Noel. My responsibility was the care of the horses. Of course Noel and I worked together, but the research and technical information I left to Noel, and once he was educated on what was available and for how much, we made the final decisions together. Besides, being involved in every single aspect was, at this stage, too demanding. We were still trying to convince four horses that we were a team and that Noel and I were the bosses!

I would rescue every horse I could, if it were possible. Noel was completely enamoured with them too, but my emotions were already out of control. So I was surprised when it was Noel that said, 'I think we need a fifth.'

'Cripes,' I said, a little overwhelmed by the thought of having another half-tonne beast to control, feed, train, and nurture.

'Don't pretend you're not thrilled,' laughed Noel. 'I knew it was a done deal as soon as I said it!'

I couldn't help but grin.

'I'll call the Association now.'

We picked up Dom just a few days later. He would be number five of our string, a 'spare wheel.' Our idea was to have one horse not carrying anything. We'd rotate the horses so they each had a few days off here and there. We also wanted to ensure all the horses could be ridden and packed, allowing us to switch them around. I was already worrying about Charlie. Ned was still extremely nervous, but I was beginning to see a change in him.

When we left to collect our fifth wheel, we thought we were collecting a horse called Beach Buggy. He was being retired from racing, and if a home wasn't found, well, his demise was on the cards.

Supposedly, Beach Buggy was a 15.1hh bay. It turned out he was a good 16.2hh - far too big for us. I was already worried about Charlie being too big at 16hh. So we said we couldn't take him. My stomach lurched in disappointment and concern. Did Beach Buggy's fate lie in our hands?

The groom disappeared while Noel and I looked at Beach Buggy.

Noel said, 'He's just too big. Charlie is going to be a struggle to pack already,'

'You're right,' I agreed sadly, my arms around my tummy, trying to contain the swirling emotions. I could feel tears pricking my eyes.

While we were dithering and worrying, the stable girl had telephoned the yard's owner. They quickly offered us Dom. He, too, had an injury that would prevent him racing: would we like him? I ummed and ahhed, worrying that a four-year-old that had never been ridden might be a bigger challenge than I could handle. Noel, however, liked him instantly. When Dom nuzzled my cheek, the deal was done.

I worried for Beach Buggy all the way home - I needn't have, as he was adopted a few days later.

Dom effortlessly slotted in with the herd but soon learned he was last in the chain of command. Being the youngest and the newest, he was put in his place. The order at the water trough clearly showed the hierarchy; Charlie was always first and allowed Ned to drink with him. Next Stevie and Spirit drank together once the first two had had their fill. After receiving a few nips, Dom quickly realised that he'd have to wait his turn and drink last.

But Dom had such a huge, fun-loving heart; he took it all in his stride. He was quite the baby, but we only gave him a few days to settle in before we started to back him.

I'd helped back horses before. However, up until Charlie I had not had the full responsibility. Charlie had taken to it very well, but I was still a bit nervous; horses can be unpredictable, and while our boys didn't seem to have a nasty bone in their bodies, their sheer weight, mixed with fear, could be lethal.

'I'd like to back Dom,' Noel said, with a conflicting note of nervousness and excitement.

'Well, okay, why not?' I could be safely on the ground while Noel took all the risks. 'We'll take it slowly,' I continued while thinking it'd be a good achievement. I felt proud of backing Charlie, and he was going great guns.

As with Charlie, we made sure Dom began to trust us first. We fed and groomed him and rubbed his itchy spots when necessary. We were having trouble with picking out his feet. He'd slam them down, or refuse to lift them when asked. He was better with his hind legs than his fronts. As well as needing him to trust us, we had to trust him; a powerful kick was something to be avoided. Noel had made it clear that if a horse ever hurt me, it'd be gone. The trouble was, if it happened you had to decipher between intent and accident.

We were quite sure Dom had no intention to hurt us, but he was becoming irritating. I wondered if he'd suffered an uncalled for whack from someone previously, as he seemed to tense when we ran our hands down his leg. So we took it slow. When he wouldn't lift a leg, or hold it up long enough for us to clean his feet, we untied him and made him walk in circles, at the end of his lead rein. This bored him silly. He couldn't eat like the others. After a few minutes, we'd try again, he'd mess about, so we'd circle him again. We repeated this until he gave in. There were no dramatics, shouting, telling off, or anger, just quiet leading and then trying again, until we had picked out his feet. His boredom levels soon became too much, and we no longer had a problem.

I taught Dom to lunge. Walking and trotting in large circles quickly becomes tedious for horses, so I kept the exercise brief. However, it encouraged Dom and the others to listen to my voice and commands. If they were a bit frisky, it was a good time for them to release some energy too.

The day came to saddle up Dom. We walked him round with the saddle buckled up on his back. He didn't worry about it one bit. We trotted him in a circle with the stirrups down, clunking at his sides, and he was fine. We then stood him beside a box.

'Stand on the box and lean on his back,' I instructed Noel.

He did, and Dom just stood there.

'Okay, lie across his back; ensure most of your weight is on your leg side. If you need to slide off, you need to do it foot-first, not head-first!' I grinned at Noel's nervous glance towards me.

'Okay, why don't you try hopping on, real slow, lower yourself gently.'

Dom was a bit surprised when Noel eventually slid into the saddle, but after that first time he was a beautiful ride. He'd occasionally give a little buck of annoyance when our leg commands became a little forceful (when he was ignoring us). He was just like a petulant child saying, 'I know!'

All the boys had learned to lunge. None of them were brilliant at it, but Spirit was the worst; he was good natured but also had strict barriers.

I lunged him one day, and he tried to pull away from me. I pulled back on his head collar. In annoyance, he swung his bottom towards me in a threatening way. He didn't kick out but definitely made the threat.

He received his first whack.

'Don't you dare do that to me!' I yelled at him. He stood with his head low, which can be a submissive indication. He had one ear pointing back showing he was listening, and hopefully having fresh regrets after my angry reaction.

'Now get out there and do more circles; we were going to stop, but now we'll start from the beginning.'

Spirit was not happy; he reluctantly continued to work, and when he hesitated I growled at him. I would be the one to decide when he could stop. He had to understand who was boss. Noel and I had to be in full control – all the time. The horses couldn't think, for one moment, that they could get the better of us. They had to trust us completely, but they also had to obey us without question – it could mean life or death out in the bush.

Aside from learning about what made the boys tick and who had which boundaries and barriers, Noel and I were truly blessed. We had become the intolerably, incessantly annoying parents who talked of nothing else but their family. Each night we repeated the day's saga to each other – even though we were both there! Our visiting friends were patient with our endless stories – 'Did you see how brave he was?'; 'He's so cheeky!'; 'They're learning so fast!' All said with prideful smiles.

It was our fifteen-year wedding anniversary. Noel told me he loved me still, and I certainly loved him. But I knew that we were both utterly and unashamedly in love with our new family.

The great thing about adoption is you are told everything you need to know – all the bad bits and all the good bits, so you know what you have. But the enormity of 'what we had' was just starting to dawn on me.

4

Whatever You Do, Don't Buy Ex-Trotters

I slumped down onto the firm grass, wrapped my arms across my knees, and cried. I looked across the yellowing grass at five horses. FIVE large, hairy, free-spirited horses! How on earth were we going to cope with five horses? The responsibility weighed me down and crumpled me into a heap. While Noel had had previous experience with horses and was now turning into a skilled 'horse-whisperer,' with more experience, I bore the brunt of the responsibility that came hand-in-hand with owning five beasts.

A few plump teardrops plopped in my lap as I chewed over the training schedule in front of us. Charlie peered at me. I hoped he would give me a hoof-hug. He blinked and lowered his head to slice through the strands of grass – Charlie's stomach was far more important to him. Eventually, I stood up and mentally and physically dusted myself off. I tidied the tack room – a good job for the soul, it helped sort out the day's muddle within the room and within my head. Lunging and schooling Dom was next. I marshalled my erratic thoughts into some sort of order; I had to get moving with the training.

The following morning, Dom played sillies as I lunged him. I allowed him his fun until he wore out; then he started to listen to me. He always approached me with head down, a submissive and respectful sign. My tears had gone, replaced with determination. A positive air accompanied me until that evening when I read the trekking manual that had just been loaned to us.

First rule: Don't make the mistake of getting ex-trotters or pacers. Everyone thinks they will be great at packing as they are used to all the gear; however, their unusual gait makes the packs bounce, which causes many problems including rubbing. After reading this peachy bit of advice and noting we had just taken on five ex-trotters, I swore, grinned, and laughed, 'Oh well, it will be an even more interesting journey.'

I put my doubts behind me and focused on the boys' good points. They were all kind; they all had their issues, emotionally, physically and mentally, but so did we. We just had to find a way to bond the team.

The first few times we took them out all together, they would shy at tree stumps and large rocks. Charlie and Ned, out front with me, set the rest off. They continued to do this, even when we had shown them, 'They're just rocks!' We realised they were not bush horses, they were too soft, and we'd have to toughen them up too.

On a particularly trying trek, the horses had jumped and skittered all day long.

'You know you said I could decide which horses would be mine?' Noel said.

'Mmmmmm,' I muttered, trying to convince Charlie that the rock he'd seen every day still wasn't going to bite him.

'Well, they're all yours today!'

I learned quickly not to tie Ned to Charlie's saddle. I had ridden and led ponies as a kid and was quite adept at handling them that way. Noel was comfortable with the other three tied together, and I'd been reading that it was possible to suffer a strain if leading with one hand all day. I wasn't sure what to do for the best, but my mind was made up for me the following day.

Riding Charlie, as an experiment, I attached Ned to Charlie's saddle. The sun's rays streaked across the blue sky, and we pushed the team up a steep hill, taking a rest where the paddock plateaued, a safe, comfortable environment. I rested my hands on the pommel of Charlie's saddle, waiting for Noel to catch up. Suddenly, Charlie darted one way and Ned swerved the other. Ned's lead rein pulled him forward, and he circled Charlie quickly. Without warning, within just a few seconds, the lead rope was wrapped around my stomach, and Charlie was still fidgeting.

'Steady, steady, easy boys,' I soothed, trying to convince them both to stand still. They stopped, and with relief and shaking hands, I extracted myself from the bounds of the rope. Ned would no longer be tied; I'd hand lead him from there on out.

All of a sudden we had a team of riding horses. At times we were like an orchestra, a symphony of leather squeaks and hoof falls, accompanied by the whispering breeze in the leaves, with the odd startled bird flapping into the air.

Noel and Stevie gelled superbly; they took care of each other. Stevie would glide forward into a sleek motion when carving a path through overgrown shrub, and Noel rode him beautifully, letting Stevie figure out the way. Spirit was content with being tied to Stevie's saddle and followed along merrily. I was handling Charlie and Ned, as they needed the most work. Dom was left to follow freely at this point.

We had our favourite riding horses but swapped them around. We thought it was important to train all five boys to be able to do everything.

However, Charlie had other ideas. When ridden, he strode out and took great pleasure in studying his surroundings, but when led, he trudged behind as if bored, whereas Ned was happy wherever he was and was great to lead.

The boys were bonding with each other too. Charlie became the leader of the five. He was gradually filling out and finding his feet. Charlie and Ned had been racing all their lives – from paddocks to the racetrack and back to paddocks. They'd seen little else; they couldn't have done because of the way Charlie behaved.

He'd look around, up hills, up to the sky, down crevices, along sheer cliff faces; he'd search and study the terrain. His behaviour made me smile. He was so enthralled, I swear he was just one moment away from galloping to the top of a hill and bursting into song: 'The hills are alive!'

With all the horses now backed and becoming accustomed to our voice commands and expectations, we decided it was time to add some new challenges. We'd be crossing many creeks on the trail. We knew Stevie would do this but had doubts about the others.

The Creek Episode

The creek was ten centimetres deep and eight metres wide, and it was time to ask our boys to cross it. Stevie had already passed this test; what we didn't realise was that we were embarking on a five-hour marathon of horses versus creeks.

You'd think it'd be a relatively easy event to convince two horses to cross a creek in order to reunite with their buddies. After all, they had settled into their new home and learned we were the herd leaders; throw in a good dollop of trust – where's the problem? Well, let me tell you...

The first idea was to talk Charlie and Ned into crossing the creek, but we had convinced neither of them this was a good idea. Ned decided to dig his heels in with as much vigour as the stubbornest mule, and Charlie had copied him – we were up against it. Cajoling, begging, arguing... was all met with a big fat, *No! No-way, no-how, nope!*

So, we conspired in a bit of trickery. Noel would ride Stevie, who crossed the creek without a second glance, and I would ride Ned. Ned would surely follow. At this point, we'd left the others in their paddock, about half a kilometre away. They were busy eating.

As per the plan, Stevie stepped across, and I was convinced Ned would follow suit. Nope! With complete and utter determination, he said, *No*. An hour of pushing, pulling, and sweet-talking didn't make the tiniest dent in his resolve.

Noel and Stevie were on one side, Ned and I on the other. I let Ned go, for we were in a small paddock and the only option, if he wanted to be with his buddy, was to cross the creek. While Ned had some time to think about this, I hot-footed back along the dirt track to collect Charlie.

Plan B – enter Charlie. Beyond the small creek that we were presently tackling, there was an appealing walk across a cool green, flat field, to another trickling creek. If we wanted to complete a loop, it'd be necessary to cross a third larger creek to reach home.

This larger creek, a massive six inches deep, was nearer the horses' paddock. It seemed a good option to try; Noel and I were already tired!

While Ned trotted up and down whinnying, Noel rode Stevie across the smaller second creek, to the larger creek, and waited there. I collected Charlie and led him down opposite Noel and Stevie. We could all hear Ned calling out, but he wouldn't cross the creek! Surely with Ned hollering and Stevie on the other side, Charlie would cross the water. Charlie dug his heels in.

Plan C – We had agreed to leave Dom in the paddock: four horses was enough to handle during this exercise, and we had no doubt that Dom would cross the creeks. I tied Charlie to a tree and collected Spirit. Spirit-the-brave crossed the creek all on his own when I asked him – off he walked, splashing his way towards Stevie and Noel without a backward glance. I could have kissed him (and probably did later). This left Charlie on the other side – alone, one ear forward, one ear back in confused contemplation. He wasn't happy about the situation, so with more gentle persuasion, he plodded on through without a drama. I tried to keep beside him, but he felt more comfortable following in my exact footsteps on the highest rocks! I was slipping and sliding and Charlie moved faster and faster – the water had a sharp chilliness that made me catch my breath. Charlie practically stamped all over me. I couldn't have been wetter if I jumped head first into a swimming pool. But I couldn't have been happier either.

That left Ned, who was not happy, half a kilometre away on his own. So Charlie, Stevie, Spirit, Noel, and a soggy me traipsed (I squelched) across the small creek, along the flat field, to find Ned neighing and watching us from the other side. He still wouldn't come over. I marched through the creek, leaving Noel with Spirit, Charlie, and Stevie. Again I attempted to cajole Ned across. By now we'd been at it for hours.

'If he won't cross a creek, he'll have to go back,' Noel said as he clenched his fists, his harsh words pushed through gritted teeth.

My heart contracted so violently I had to catch my breath; if I lost Ned, I'd lose Charlie too – they went everywhere together. I frowned and struggled with Ned even more. He lowered his head and literally rammed me out of the way. He did it gently, as though he didn't want to hurt me, but with determined force.

'We have to find someone who can teach these horses to do what we want,' Noel called out, dripping with exasperation. I was sad before; now I was angry. Noel was saying I wasn't up to it! I would show him, and I slapped Neddy hard on his rump. His eyes bulged, and he cowered. Watching Ned's fear, my actions simultaneously sickened me; the brutal regret clutched my heart. My sadness and anger held hands and invited desolation along to join them in an emotional drowning.

Telling Neddy off created more problems: he tried to make himself smaller, as though he expected another smack. I'll never forget this moment for the rest of my life. How my behaviour was so inconceivably and utterly wrong. How despairingly mean I was. I prayed Neddy would one day forgive me.

Ned and I needed a time-out. We skirted the paddock and calmly stood together, having a little chat. I apologised and made a big fuss of my sweet, scared boy. Meanwhile, Noel found another crossing that was slightly narrower and not in the shadows of a canopy of trees.

'Hey, how about trying here? It's not so dark.'

Ned and I walked over to where Noel was pointing. 'I don't know.' I looked at the weedy course down to the new section Noel had suggested. It was awkward: a slither of pathway, rapidly declining, slippery and yet another challenge. 'Well, we'll try,' I said doubtfully.

Ned and I slid down the bank together. Ned confidently followed me along the track, but as I stepped in the water, I slipped, which made him jump backwards. With an inward groan, I stopped and took some time to settle him back down. For some reason, I thought that undoing his reins was a good idea at this point – if anything happened (and I had a feeling it would) his leg wouldn't catch in them.

I sucked in a fortifying breath and walked back into the creek with Ned following me! Once he realised he was in up to his knees, he galloped as fast as he possibly could through the creek toward his buddies. Leaving me standing in the middle of the creek, boots filling with water, dripping from the splashes Ned had kicked up. Beneath the drenching, I wore a huge grin.

The horses bucked, cavorted, and shook their heads in celebration. Never had I seen horses so damned proud of themselves. We let them play and eat. I needed to drip dry and recoup my waning energy reserves. We had to cross at least one creek to get them back home.

Stevie was the expert, with Spirit hot on his heels. They plodded back through without a drama. Charlie hesitated, snorted, and plunged in, closely followed by Ned with a less worrisome face; Stevie and Spirit were awarded the brave-heart awards; Charlie and Ned won 'getting braver-heart' awards. Noel won the patient award, and I won the soggy, emotional, and perseverance award. They had an extra handful of feed that evening. So did Noel and I! I was incredibly proud.

Dom embraced all the challenges without question, which was why we'd left him in the paddock. We continued to pack Stevie and Spirit. They were wonderfully calm as we plonked strange, colourful bags on their backs.

Ned and Charlie were a different story. I was starting to realise that Charlie was the largest in size and the biggest coward. I loved him to bits, but even Ned would lose his patience with him. At an unexpected noise or quick movement, Charlie and Ned would stop. Ned would listen to me, trust me, and when I asked him to walk-on, he would – then Charlie would be brave enough to follow Ned – this did create some problems as I was riding Charlie more than I was Ned. It was as if Ned had lost the energy for neat adrenaline rushes at every moment and felt safe in my hands.

During this time, I was publishing my first book. Internet was scratchy at Kangaroo Valley, and I needed to arrange the front covers and formatting. One afternoon, I drove into Nowra, forty minutes away.

In the morning, I had spent some time with Ned. I lunged him, but then we rode out together. As we walked past Andrea's car on our way back, he snorted and tensed. I dismounted and led him over to the car. Gently, calmly, I leaned my back against the vehicle and talked to Ned.

'It's okay, what's to worry about?' Ned leaned his head against my tummy as I stroked his ears. He sucked in and breathed out the largest sigh I'd ever heard. It was an exhale of relief, but also letting go. He let go bound muscles; his furrowed brows smoothed. For the first time since he arrived, he was totally relaxed and at peace - he was home. His whole demeanour changed that morning, and it brought tears to my eyes.

That afternoon, driving back to Kangaroo Valley, the morning with Ned returned to my mind vividly. We had a 'moment' together, a real connection. I burst into tears. I knew then that I was in trouble. I calmed down and reached home, but when I saw Noel, I cried again.

'I can't ever let these boys go,' I sobbed, 'I love them too much!' Noel folded me within his thick arms while I told him the story of Ned.

'It's okay, we'll figure something out,' he said, pushing back my hair and peering at my tear-smudged face. 'If we have to go to the UK for a while, we'll work it out.' Personal events were calling me back to England. I wasn't ready to go, but I knew I would in the future; I wanted to at some point, but now it had become complicated.

My dad had been unwell, and it had been quite some time since our last visit. We'd planned to go to the UK after our trekking adventure, spending time with my immediate family. Friends would care for the horses as I reconnected back home. Those plans were in our heads for a year or two in the future, but already it seemed too soon, too frightening.

Bucking and Farting

We had established a rough routine. Four days a week Noel and I worked, teaching maritime in the evenings. Most of the mornings were clear to spend time with the boys, the afternoons free for preparing for class and the evening's lesson.

Usually, we'd take a short ride or just bring them in for a groom. Working Monday through to Thursday meant we had three clear days at the weekend to hike out with the string of five.

We'd often trek out with Noel on Stevie and Spirit tied to his saddle. Spirit would be packed up with two empty plastic panniers. Tied to him was Dom, who we hadn't packed yet.

I rode Charlie, and we tried Ned with packs. We had two sets of the plastic panniers, two large canvas bags, and saddle-bags for the ridden horses. Before we introduced Ned to the canvas bags, we clipped on the small saddle-bags. It was like clipping on hand bags!

The boys understood their roles, and Noel's string of three led in a line beautifully, Spirit's head at Stevie's flank and Dom's head at Spirit's flank. Each lead rope was just long enough for Spirit and Dom to pick at the grass when we stopped, but not too long so they could tread on it or get their legs caught. It was a striking sight, such contented, happy horses.

Ned didn't like the pack-saddle. It clunked and jingled, and he wore his worried face when we put it on. As soon as it stopped clunking, he relaxed. Noel and I saddled him up together; he was quite flighty, and we didn't want him taking off. He accepted his hand bags easily as they were soft and didn't make noise. The canvas bags were the next step; he wasn't sure, but once they were in place he relaxed. It was the noise he didn't like.

Charlie was ridden mostly, but we had tried the small saddle-bags (hand bags) on him, and he accepted them without too much of a drama.

We knew Stevie packed okay, so we tried Dom with the noisy plastic panniers; he didn't worry one bit. Our team was taking shape!

I experienced such a great thrill riding Charlie; he was finally putting on weight and gaining a shine to his coat, his muscles pushing against his skin; you could see he felt fit, head high, gleaming, interested eyes. He continued to view his surroundings with curiosity. Kangaroo Valley is hilly, and some rises were quite steep. Trekking along the dirt trails, Charlie would peer up the incline beside us. I could almost hear him ask, *Can we run up it? Can we? Can we please?* He'd turn towards the foot of the hill and speed up as if I wouldn't notice! I'd always answer his questions with 'no,' since our usual ride encompassed enough hills.

Occasionally, Noel and I would have two horses each and leave the fifth to roam freely. One day I rode Ned and led Dom, with packs on. Noel rode Stevie and led a packed Spirit.

Charlie was following, and he thought this was a great lark. He swung his enormous head in a large arc, kicked up his heels, and galloped off at every paddock we trekked through. After a few bucks, he'd stop, realise he'd left the others, and trot back to us wearing the cheekiest grin. Tail up high, head even higher, he'd flick his nose out in full show-off mode. Seeking out a patch of grass, he'd then embark on a quick munch. Suddenly, as we gained a few hundred metres on him, his head would fly up, and he'd leap up and gallop after us, bucking and farting with glee. He certainly was a happy horse.

I'm convinced he was a bit depressed when he arrived. You could almost see him thinking, *Another change, another move, another person to try to understand – will I be safe?* After a few weeks he was settling, and as he was allowed to be himself, he indulged, showing his true, mischievous character. I just hoped he never comprehended his own power: at 16hh, filling out and muscling up, he was a power-house. He didn't own an evil bone in his huge, square body. In fact, if he had a small cut that needed treatment, he became the biggest coward. I would spray antiseptic lotion on a small nick on his hind leg. He'd lift his leg, not a threat, but from fear; he didn't try to kick me, but the leg was up, and he looked at me as if to say, *Sorry, but I'm scared, I can't help it!* I told him off with just a couple of stern words, and I tapped his leg.

'Put it down, Charlie.'

He sulked thereafter; he hated being told off. Carrots and hugs soon won him over, and we found a happy compromise, I agreed not to spray lotion on him, but to dab it carefully.

We were still nursing Ned; he was becoming quite affectionate with us. I am sure he was appreciating being given a chance – that's all he needed, a bit of patience. However, he still spooked easily. I spent hours with him, showing him how the bags wouldn't hurt him. Placing them on his back, letting them slide off. After a long session he would relax, but every time I brought the bags out, on a different day, he tensed, and we started again. Gradually, though, he accepted the equipment; he wasn't too chuffed if a branch scraped against his bags. But he trusted us... until it all hurtled completely out of control.

7

Charlie The Saboteur

Noel was strapping the second canvas bag on Ned while I held him. He was calm, and we thought we'd cracked it. Maybe we relaxed a bit too much. Suddenly his muscles bunched, and before we could finish clipping on the last strap, he took off. The bag slipped part-way down his tummy and jangled noisily. He freaked.

Noel stepped back, and I stupidly tried to hang onto the rope. In an instant, my mind raced forward, watching a loose, panicky horse. *He's going to run through a fence and kill himself*, I thought. As the fear engulfed Ned, he dropped his head and kicked out backwards, trying to throw the noisy, frightening gear off himself. I ducked just in time and let go of the rope, watching with utter despair as he galloped off. There was nothing we could do.

Ned galloped away from us, bucking like a true bronco. Suddenly he stopped, spun on his heels, and came right back at us, full pelt. The other boys were tied to a fence, watching, intrigued. Ned galloped hell-for-leather straight at Noel and me. Like two cartoon characters, we scattered just in time. I watched in horror as Ned hurtled towards a steep drop-off. Just in the nick of time, he applied the brakes, stopped, spun around, and galloped back past us. He headed up towards his paddock gate, his head between his knees and his back legs in the air. I have no idea how he galloped so fast with his arched back. Every buck loosened the bags more, which created more noise, which in turn made him buck harder.

I followed Ned up the hill, and fortunately he stopped in a corner. Great wafts of steam spread from his nostrils with each ragged blow. His white eyes were popping while his sweat-caked coat steamed.

'It's okay, Ned, Neddy boy, good boy,' I soothed. He let me approach him. I kept calm, talking, patting, reassuring. He was rigid, a snorting steam train; the slightest noise and he'd explode again. Noel caught up with us and helped settle Neddy too. We unclipped the bags without further problems.

Andrea stepped out of her house to see what all the commotion was. I felt compelled to apologise. It was dangerous, a wild horse going berserk around her property. As usual, Andrea offered us all the support we needed. A crazed, lunatic, half-tonne beast careening around her property didn't faze her one bit! It took a while for my adrenaline to stop galloping though.

We were right back where we started with Ned.

We all took a few days off from packing. We rode the boys and avoided all the pack-saddles. We then turned our attention to Charlie; he'd only carried the small saddle-bags so far. Noel was convinced he would be fine, but I wasn't so sure. We strapped on the canvas bags, and although a bit startled, he begrudgingly accepted them.

'Ned and Charlie can't have it all their own way,' said Noel, running his hands through his hair. 'We need to have at least one of them carry the hard plastic panniers.'

These panniers sounded like drums and worried me. I knew Charlie would protest.

'Charlie will be fine,' Noel said. 'Let's load him up.'

With two plastic panniers half-clipped on, Charlie took off, streaking across the paddock, panniers flapping at his side. The terror painted on his face broke my heart as he headed full pelt for the fence. He didn't buck – he was galloping too hard. I could only watch and wait for him to kill himself. I called him, I begged him, and he too ran straight for us! We were standing with the other boys. Noel and I dived out of the way. Before he leaped down a huge embankment, where he'd surely break his legs, he stopped and just puffed. As with Neddy, we calmly released him. He blew out his adrenaline and started eating hay. He'd be fine, but I doubted if I'd ever recover.

We made the decision to pursue the bags with Ned and leave Charlie as a riding horse. He was so tall, it was a struggle to lift the bags on together. Ned listened to us more and wanted to overcome his fears. Charlie was either fine or in a blind panic; there seemed to be no middle ground.

To help us prepare the other four, we let Charlie roam freely once again. He loved his freedom, and quite often he'd trot out in front, leading the herd. He'd hike up a hill in front of us, have a good look around, then come back down, as if scouting for the enemy. I was coping well with Ned and Dom. Dom was great at being led. Ned was relaxing and a joy to ride, with his eager and sure footing. Noel rode Stevie, a great team. Spirit, our cool dude, became utterly content to be led.

Leading horses while riding was new to Noel, but he was doing well until Charlie started to interfere. Charlie would walk in step beside me and my two and not cause any trouble. However, he'd then decide trot up to Noel, slow to a walk, then wedge himself between Noel's two horses. He'd push them apart with his massive shoulders. With Spirit's lead rope taut between him and Stevie, Noel would cuss at Charlie. Charlie would then extract himself, but as he cleared Noel's troop he'd turn ninety degrees in front of Stevie and steer him into the bank (at least it wasn't the other way, to the two hundred metre drop!). Charlie would just stop, block the way, and refuse to move. I am sure he then looked at me to see how hard I was laughing. I have no idea what was going on in his mind, except he was hell-bent on sabotaging Noel and his two boys. As Charlie came my way once again, he'd just walk alongside me, on a pleasant country stroll, with no problems whatsoever. After five or ten minutes, he'd get another twinkle in his eye and take off towards Noel, and I'd hear, 'NOOOOO, just fuck off, Charlie!'

I, of course, ended up in a heap, giggling my head off, clutching my cramping tummy.

'It's not fucking funny,' Noel would scream. 'Get your bloody horse under control!'

Alas, I wasn't allowed to let Charlie roam free any more. Both Charlie and I missed those moments.

Noel didn't.

8

Horses Training Us!

On the whole they are all good, I said to myself with a satisfied smile and settled back into daily training. Spring arrived with a rich flourish; new grass and bright days provided renewed energy for us all. Noel and I had finished the drudge and distraction of work. We could now focus on the team full time.

Being an employee and working for someone else is not something I do easily. I fall into good jobs, I earn well, but I dislike it immensely. I liked teaching though, and I felt such a sense of achievement from being a trainer, but the expectations of conforming to staid rules within the workplace, the corporate pandering, the stiff suits - it suffocates me, it restricts, and leaves me with a constant muzzy head. I rebel, and at times I am lucky I have good skills to keep me employed when I want to be. I'm not good at following rules. Now, I was ecstatic to be making all the rules: I just hoped I was making the right ones!

Stevie developed a small cough, so when we turfed them out in the paddock I spent some time feeling glands, checking the colour of the discharge from his nose, and listening to his breathing. I talked to him, calmly stroking his cheeks. Usually he fell asleep when I did this, but this time his eyes were closing and suddenly *chomp* – he bit down on my hand! I was shocked and took a step back. Stevie jumped away from me, knowing he was in trouble.

'He just bit me!'

Stevie took off with the rest of the herd, galloping, high-tailed, in his footsteps. My hand was bruised, and I bit my lip, trying hard not to cry again. All the love I gave them, the time, the care, and money, and this was what they gave me in return.

Spirit had been grumpy too. He had pulled threatening faces at me when I asked him to move aside when brushing him down. With all these thoughts, my heart sank. The emotional roller-coaster twisted at full pelt.

'Perhaps we have to remember,' Noel said gently, 'that they are just dumb animals.'

Spirit had shown us his boundaries, with warnings. Stevie had made it clear that his time in the paddock was his own. But we had to have one hundred percent trust between us all, or we'd have problems away from home. Stevie's cough soon settled, and we put it down to heightened pollen at springtime.

Noel had hurt his back and was flat-out on the sofa while I lunged all five animals (one at a time). They did a good job, and I indulged in a little satisfaction, but the whole undertaking was still prodding in my mind with a stab of doubt. With the boys back out in their paddock, and making an effort to allay my fears, I pulled off my boots and stepped into our cottage, clumps of hay clinging to my socks. I sat opposite Noel with a heady blend of fulfilment and fatigue.

'I've been studying the guides,' Noel said from his prone position. He'd been reading avidly while letting his back repair. 'The trail sounds exciting.'

It had better be, I thought. *Right now I need some more incentives!* The roller coaster ride of emotions was hurtling up mountains one minute and down into ditches the next.

Once Noel was in better shape, the seven of us went out together most days. We'd often ride with Andrea; her boys had met new challenges too. She had convinced them to traverse the creeks as well. We all enjoyed each other's company. Andrea's good poise made her a natural rider.

As we strode along the soft, rutted path, enjoying the peace, quiet, and safety of riding on private land, we updated Andrea on our exploits.

'The boys are learning well; they seem to understand who goes in front of who at each gate and so forth,' Noel explained proudly. Without conscious thought, his body was finely in tune with Stevie's; they moved as one.

'That's just great,' Andrea said. 'They seem to be adapting to the packs too.'

'Yup, we are making progress!'

We reached a gate, and Noel hopped off Stevie, leaving his three standing. He pulled the gate towards him. Andrea was behind with her two, and I was up the rear with Charlie and Ned.

Stevie decided to pick this moment to show us up, and I am sure all our boys were in cahoots.

'Whooa, no. Stand, Stevie,' Noel called in an authoritative manner. Stevie stopped, and Spirit did too, but Dom was too busy looking at a pretty bird and walked into Spirit's rump. Spirit's ears shot back, and he walked forward. His line tugged on Stevie, who walked forward to the gate.

'Back, back, BAAAACK!' Noel was losing his patience; he had three of them to push back now.

Eventually, they moved back enough to allow him to open the gate, and he led them through and kept walking.

'I'll do the gate,' Andrea said, already half out of her saddle.

'Nah, that's okay, it'll be easier if I do it,' I called out, for the path was narrow enough to cause a tangle of horses if we started turning them around.

I flicked Ned's lead rope over his neck and hopped off Charlie while I was waiting for Noel. As I walked through the gate, something spooked Charlie and Ned, and they took off. I kept hold of Charlie, but Ned barged his way between Noel (and his three) and Andrea (and her two); then Ned was trapped. With nowhere to go horizontally, he went vertically; he turned into a bucking bronco maniac.

There was nothing we could do but watch.

'Neddy, Neddy-boy, it's okay.' We all cooed, but I noticed with a detached air of amusement, that none of us was particularly worried. Ned had nowhere to go. He was literally going vertical, up and down on all fours with a wonderfully curved back. He jumped and hopped, and we waited for him to wear himself out.

'Good boy, Neddy, you're okay,' I said soothingly, smiling at him. He finally stopped his leaping, heaved a big sigh, and looked around as if to say, *Whoah! What was all that about?*

His bags hadn't moved, he wasn't hurt, and he had forgotten what had set him off. He looked at us sheepishly, as if a little embarrassed. We gave him a minute to catch his breath and level out his adrenaline. I closed the gate, and we mounted up and carried on.

'Honestly, Andrea, it was all going so well!' Noel said with his hand on the back of his neck.

Noel had a great thing going with his gang of three. They looked professional. Meanwhile, I had problems with Ned and Charlie; we had to get one of them packing. After the last debacle, everyone was nervous, but we took our time with Ned and practiced each day. We worked hard to reassure him, and soon he accepted it – he didn't like it, but he accepted it. Again, we started him with small bags and then larger ones. He was becoming proficient, and I am sure he was proud of himself, that he was conquering his fear. Spirit and Dom carried the hard panniers, and we kept the soft panniers for Ned, as they made less noise.

Noel and I continually fought with the plastic panniers; they were cumbersome and heavy. We both needed to lift them on together. During our sailing days, and throughout any challenge we take on, both Noel and I like to be independent. We each enjoy the journey far more if we are capable of coping on our own – if we need to. It made sense, both for our own satisfaction and safety, to be able to handle every aspect. The canvas bags didn't hold as much as the panniers, so we had to persevere. We didn't have time to think of new solutions. Besides, we had spent weeks researching what was out there, and there was little other choice.

The training ground at Kangaroo Valley was ideal; we completed several one-day trips up a steep hill, a four-hour ride where there was little clue provided to identify which century we were in. We carried hay for the horses and a snack-picnic for us. At the top of the paddock, the boys gratefully munched the hay, and we ate lunch. Charlie was more interested in our tuna sandwiches. Knowing food was in abundance, he ignored the hay and wandered off on his own. Periodically he'd glance back, checking that the rest of us were where he'd left us, and then he'd continue to look around. There were ravines to explore, hills and paths leading to who knew where. He just loved investigating! Noel and I kept hold of the other boys; we didn't need them all gallivanting around on their own.

With most of our gear organised, Noel was busy sorting through what we had and noting what else we needed. This left Andrea and I to indulge in a quiet ride together. She brought along Cedar and Jet, and I took Ned and Charlie. I decided to ride Ned for a change and lead Charlie, without any packs.

As we quietly padded up overgrown passages and down ravines, breathing in the earthy scents, a few light drops of liquid fell on my face.

'How can it be raining?' I asked. 'There's not a cloud in the sky.'

'Oh, don't worry, that's just the cicadas peeing on you!' Andrea grinned.

How lovely! I thought sarcastically. Cicadas are insects, best known for the reverberating, incessant noise made by the males at dusk.

There were two trickling creeks to cross on the way home. All the boys strode through without a second thought, but when Ned marched up the bank I felt him hobble.

'Here, grab Charlie for a minute; something's up with Ned.' I led Ned away and trotted him; he was sound in walk and in trot.

'Is his head bobbing in the trot?' I asked Andrea. Horses' heads stay perfectly still in trot, so it's easy to see if they are lame. Their head will bob in degrees of intensity to the pain.

'I don't think so; let's swap and you have a look.'

'Hmm, you're right,' I said, feeling my brow crease with concentration. 'I think he's okay, just one of those things.' With relief, we both mounted back up and carried on the pleasant sojourn in company of a sunny August day.

We had booked a truck to take us to Aberdeen, NSW in a few days. We didn't need injuries to cause delays. The next day Ned was lame.

'I can't see or feel anything,' I said desperately, running my hands up and down his legs. 'There's no apparent bruising, or cut; no bumps, nothing.'

At the same time, two friends, Mick and Lynne, came for a visit. Mick had some experience with horses; both he and Andrea took a look at Ned's leg and couldn't see any signs of injury either.

'I'll bandage the lower leg for support just in case,' I said, flicking the catches on the red first aid kit. 'We'll see how he is tomorrow.'

'We'd better delay the truck,' Noel said.

Our farrier was due to come out for the horses' final trim. He was a barefoot farrier and whole-heartedly supported what we were doing. He had spent the last few months trimming their feet to help shape them correctly. We were not shoeing our boys.

'It's probably a bruised foot,' he explained. This made sense, as the creek's bed was lined with small rocks. We couldn't see any bruising, but Clive, the owner of the land, had some experience previously with cows bruising their feet.

'Yup, I'd say it was a bruised foot,' he agreed.

We rested Ned and delayed the truck driver.

While our boys were standing together, munching hay, Mick and I were looking at them. Mick had owned horses previously and was intrigued; he was comfortable around them. After looking at Ned, we were all standing about four metres off to Spirit's right-hand side. He was at a right angle to us.

Spirit had become grumpy with me. I regularly picked ticks off him, and he grew to hate it. I could understand why, but it was hard to leave those evil creatures half-buried in his skin! With his ears pinned back and throwing his nose out towards me, Spirit told me in no uncertain terms that he wanted to be left alone. Spirit and I weren't getting on; I wouldn't put up with him being moody and making half-threats; he had to respect me.

Mick, Noel, Lynne, and I looked at Spirit and pointed to him. He was well aware we were talking about him. Without warning, his back leg flew out towards us in obvious anger. We were too far away for it to be anywhere near us.

'Oh my God,' Mick said, his eyes almost popping out. 'I've never seen a horse do that before!' He giggled nervously.

Noel and I laughed too, but we knew Spirit; we weren't so nervous. I hadn't seen a horse do that either, but he knew we were too far away. He was just sick and tired of being picked at. He liked attention but not fuss; he was saying, *Okay, I've had enough, I am okay, leave me alone.*

Eventually, Spirit had me trained, and he forgave my picking sessions; we became buddies again. Spirit loved his role of packing; he was content and playful, but at the end of the day, that time was his, and he was let be. We'd all worked through and ironed out each of our own little quirks; the relationships between us all were understood, appreciated, secure. Spirit and Noel's bond only grew. I am sure the pair of them had secret conversations. With Spirit in tow, when Noel stopped Stevie, Spirit would gently place his head on Noel's knee and look up at him. Often, he'd stick out his tongue. If Noel ignored him, he'd slide his head off Noel's leg and put the top of his head on the bottom of Noel's foot. He'd then proceed to lift Noel's leg with his head. He was playing, for it was gentle, but if Spirit got carried away he'd almost flip him out of the saddle!

Ned's little quirk was swinging his round bottom towards you. It looked like he was threatening to kick, but he wanted his tail scratched. He adored a good rub, and, of course, I would indulge him. If I was anywhere near him, he'd swing his big behind in my direction. These boys had me right where they wanted me.

By now we had our tent, a two-man tent with a vestibule. The packing gear would stack up beneath the small entrance at night and keep dry. We had no excuse: it was time to do a proper run for a few nights, away from the house and all its comforts.

We planned to camp in a paddock about twenty minutes from the cottages, then climb a steep hill the following day and camp again. We packed up all the gear. It took us five hours!

'We'll get better at it,' Noel said when I frowned in dismay.

It was late; fortunately we had a short journey. The seven of us padded along the dirt track that was so familiar to us all, and soon we were unpacking and pitching the tent. We carried an electric fence and plastic poles. The horses stood in their new paddock munching dinner after drinking their fill of water.

'I've forgotten the matches!' Noel said, his hand on his head as if to pull out some hair. 'I don't believe it!'

I grinned as I watched him sigh and throw a wave over his shoulder as he trotted back up to the house.

As the evening sloped in we lit a fire, drank a glass of wine, and relaxed - *This was easy*, we thought.

Before we turned in, we wandered over to check the boys. Charlie and Ned nuzzled our pockets for treats but soon left when they realised we had none. Spirit made it perfectly clear with flat-back ears that we should not intrude – fair enough, it was his time. All further inspections would be made from outside their fence!

After deep comfortable sleeps, we awoke at dawn, ready for day two. With few accessible trees to tie to, it was tricky to manage all five horses and pack up. We'd forgotten the luxury of using a fence each day by the cottage.

I had made hobbles for each horse, to enable us to let the boys go and keep them nearby. I hated these contraptions. When I put them on, the horses looked at me as if to say, *You're kidding*. They tripped, stumbled, and fell, and I knew they hated them too. Slowly we hauled our gear onto their backs and saddled up our mounts. As we were almost done, I unbuckled the hobbles. Then something spooked them.

Spirit took off with his panniers only half clipped on; as he ran, the plastic containers jumped up and down on his back and rattled. This didn't faze him, but Dom started running because of the noise, and Spirit in turn was trying to keep up with Dom! With Spirit's equipment clattering and Spirit hot on Dom's heels, the noise only made Dom go faster!

Charlie and Stevie took off in pursuit, as it seemed good fun, and Ned had no idea what was going on, so he ran straight up to me! We watched as Spirit jangled along and the others tried to run away from him, while he kept trying to catch them. There was nothing we could do but laugh. Eventually the horses seemed to figure out what was going on – they stopped and started to eat. We rounded them up and continued packing.

Eventually we were on our way; the steep climb would take four hours with regular pit stops. We crossed the creek as if we'd been doing it for years, and the boys stretched out into a healthy stride. We took our time. The team was fit, with developed hind muscles. But they were carrying us, and gear and the climb was relentless.

We decided to camp at a different paddock, one we hadn't found before, and so we took paths that we didn't know. Then disaster struck.

9

Snapped Leg

Noel was in front, riding Stevie with Spirit and Dom behind. Spirit was fully packed up, but Dom carried a lighter load, though his muscles were almost ready for a full load. I was riding Charlie and leading Ned, who was also fully packed. We were riding along a narrow path and had stepped over a fallen tree. The tree was adolescent in size, and there were two forked branches to step over, both just a few inches thick. They stepped over one branch, then the other. We had done this once already: we were doubling back as the better camping spot was half a kilometre back. We turned around. As Stevie stepped over the branches, Spirit became stuck.

'Stop, stop,' I yelled. I could see Spirit's hoof caught between the branches. Noel stopped Stevie and leaped off. Stevie seemed to know what was going on. (Noel constantly dismounted and just left him; he didn't wander, just waited patiently where he was left.) Noel raced up to Spirit, and as I called out, 'Do you need a hand?' Spirit started to go down.

'Yes, yes, help, HELP,' screamed Noel, and the thud of dread hit the pit of my stomach. Noel doesn't panic and had never screamed for help.

As I jumped off Charlie and slung Ned's rope over his neck, I could see Spirit's leg folding beneath him, and Noel trying to hold him up. Spirit's nose dug into the ground, and he groaned loudly. Noel was crying, 'No, no.' I couldn't see why until I crouched next to Spirit. His front leg was bent at an impossible angle. His leg had snapped. I screamed.

I felt like I needed to vomit, and tears streamed down my face. Horrific solutions stormed through my mind. We had to put this guy out of his misery as soon as possible. We were an hour away from the cottages if I moved fast with one horse. We were near the top of an incredibly steep hill, we had five horses, and it was getting late. But I *had* to do something. With my heart shattering into painful shards, I checked the leg again. From the fetlock down, the leg was bent forward; it was broken for sure. No blood. Spirit expelled a deep, painful moan. Tears ran down Noel's cheeks, and I was enfolded within a chill of doom.

'Get his gear off his back, talk to him, tell him how much we love him, make him comfortable; I'm taking Stevie and getting a gun!'

Blinded by tears, I whipped off Stevie's saddle-bags and leaped up on him.

'Be careful,' Noel called. I had no stirrups, I couldn't adjust Noel's short enough for me, and I didn't want to waste time changing saddles. Spirit was in great pain; I had to do something right now.

Charlie and Ned stood rooted to the spot, near Dom, as if sensing something sickening was happening. Ned had sidled right up to Charlie for comfort. Noel started to unpack Spirit. I turned Stevie towards home and eased him forward with my legs.

Stevie hates leg commands, so I just let him go; I let him decide the speed downhill. He knew it was an emergency; he could sense my angst. He galloped like the wind when it was safe and steadied to a trot when it was steep and stony. I clung on. Between gasping tears, I reassured him and provided encouragement. Then the picture of Spirit's leg would flash in my mind.

'Oh, God, what have I done?'

'I shouldn't have gone up that path.'

'What was I thinking, to imagine we could do this?'

'I'm sorry, Spirit. I am so, so sorry.'

I sobbed all the way down the hill.

I realised that maybe I had bitten off more than I could chew. Stevie sensed my fear as we plunged down the mountain trail.

I tried to focus on the task at hand. I had to relieve Spirit's pain. Ragged breaths rapidly spurted from both horse and rider's nostrils. I clutched Stevie's mane for more balance as he leaped up steep banks, leaving curtains of creek water dripping from his legs.

Sweat flowed, tears streamed, and sobs escaped via my aching heart.

We reached the last creek; Stevie and I were puffing hard, and the sun was still beating its warmth down. We traversed the stream through the deepest part and galloped up the hill to Clive and Andrea's cottage.

'Get a gun,' I yelled. 'Spirit's broken his leg!'

Clive looked up from his veranda, smiled, and waved.

'I'm not joking; get a bloody gun NOW!' Another wave from Clive and an uncomfortable shifting in seats from his two guests beside him. I'd reached their gate and heard Andrea say, 'Did you hear what she said? Spirit's broken his leg!'

'Shit,' I heard Clive say, and he raced off in one direction to find his gun, then cursing the rules of owning firearms, he pelted in another direction to retrieve the bullets.

I told Stevie how wonderful he was, took off his gear, and let him drink steadily – I put him in the paddock with Andrea's boys, but he wanted his other mates; he stood at the gate and watched me collapse in a heap while I waited for Clive to put his gun together.

Andrea and the guests (another couple) gathered around me while I sobbed out the story.

We all bundled in the Land Cruiser Troop. Clive pushed down on the accelerator. 'Hang on, it'll be a bumpy ride!' He continued a personal monologue about the 'foolish rules' of gun keeping as we battled along the rough terrain, climbing steep inclines, powering along ravines, and pushing through creeks. Clive was a marvel at the wheel, stopping to move large rocks along the way. We all clung to the truck, pale, shocked – all hoping we'd wake up from this nightmare.

As Clive gunned the engine to attack the last hill, I glanced to my left. There stood Noel and three horses: Stevie, Dom, and Spirit. Was it Spirit? Or was it Charlie? They were the same colour. *Oh God*, I thought, *where's Spirit?*

'Stop the car; there they are!' I yelled. Clive braked, and I thoughtlessly trampled over everyone to get out.

'Careful, wait!' Clive called, while trying to avoid my heavy boots. But I couldn't. I sprinted to Noel, and there stood Spirit.

Spirit stood there, yes, stood.

Noel grabbed me, and we clung to each other sobbing, gasping.

'What happened?'

'I unloaded his gear, and he just stood up!'

'How could he? How could he?' I gasped.

Noel just shrugged.

The others joined us, and we stood together, totally perplexed.

'I know what I saw,' Noel said, scratching his head as if it would help him recall.

'It must be a miracle,' Andrea said quietly, as perplexed as we were.

And, my goodness, what else could it have been?

We regrouped. Spirit's leg was swelling, two horses were missing, and it was getting late. Half our gear was somewhere up a hill too, strewn in different places as Noel had also unloaded Dom as he led them down the track.

Clive and his guests retrieved our equipment while Andrea and I bandaged Spirit's legs. I didn't think the first aid kit would be put to use on the second day of trekking! We bandaged all four legs to provide support on the hill for the journey down. Then, while Andrea stayed with Spirit, Dom, and Stevie, Noel and I searched for Charlie and Ned. They had wandered off after following Noel down the hill.

'Where the devil are they?' I asked no one in particular, pushing thistles aside with my boot.

'Why would they just wander off on their own; what were they thinking?'

We walked in the direction Noel had seen them go. After an hour, we turned back.

'I wonder if they've become confused, thinking this was the way home – they haven't passed us,' I said thoughtfully, trying to look beyond the hills and through the bush. 'I bet they've gone back to where Spirit went down.'

Noel rolled his eyes. We trudged back up the hill using reserves of energy we didn't know we had, and there they stood – quietly, together, exactly where I'd left them before I jumped on Stevie. Their kind faces held the relief of seeing us; mine reflected that relief back.

We didn't know what to do, they seemed to say.

Noel, Andrea, and I led all five of them slowly down the hill. Spirit wasn't lame, but I knew there'd be trouble with that leg tomorrow. A hush hung over the group; the thundering emotions and disbelief encouraged our silence but sucked all our energy.

Noel and I had seen the ugly twist in Spirit's leg. We did not become that emotional without good reason – I certainly wouldn't have risked Stevie to fetch a gun if I didn't think the injury had been fatal.

The next day he was lame, bruised, swollen, and stiff. We hosed him down several times a day and talked incessantly about what had happened.

Noel and I were shattered; I felt grey and drained. We fed the horses silently and led them to the paddock. We were dehydrated, exhausted, and emotionally wrecked, but we hadn't shot our horse – it had been too close. Spirit's lameness would delay us, but he quickly repaired and became stronger and stronger. He and Noel developed a remarkable bond. Spirit had known he was in trouble; maybe he thought we'd saved his life, when in fact we had almost ended it! I still feel sick to my stomach when I think about that day. I think it took Noel and I a lot longer than Spirit to recover.

10

Choking

I rang the truck driver again to try to postpone our start for the second time. Spirit was still bruised and slightly lame, but he improved each day. He was a solid horse, fit and immensely healthy, which helped the healing. But the truck driver was not happy.

'Horses are resilient, you know,' he said sharply. 'He will probably be fine.'

The vivid pictures of his mangled leg seeped back into my mind, horrifying me all over again.

'Okay, we can stop at the first camp a week or so when we arrive, so he can rest there too,' I said reluctantly. 'Let's stick with the same date.'

Jet and Cedar, Andrea's two boys, were getting in the swing of our training, and Jet particularly enjoyed the outings; he was becoming fit too. When we took our team without him and Andrea, he'd watch for us at the gate, calling at times.

'I've been thinking about Spirit and his leg,' said Andrea to us one day as the departure date was drawing near. She'd watched me worry and wonder whether I was doing the right thing.

'I'd like to offer Jet to you,' she said kindly.

'For the trip?' I asked, surprised. I shouldn't have been so shocked: Andrea is one of the most generous people I know.

'I know you are worried about Spirit; if you think Jet could handle it, and you'd like to, I'll swap Jet for Spirit for a while.'

Noel and I were overwhelmed by such a magnificent offer. Andrea loved her boys – her proposal was not made lightly.

'Thank you so much, that is immensely kind,' Noel said, mirroring my thoughts and meeting Andrea's eyes in earnest.

'Yes, thank you!' I said. 'I actually think Spirit will be okay; he's pretty much sound now and seems quite happy to take weight on his leg when we pick out his other feet.'

'Also,' said Noel, 'we'd have to train Jet in packing pretty quick. I tell you what, if anything else goes wrong, you may have a deal, but at the moment, we'll stick with the plan.'

'Okay, but the offer's there.'

The boys gelled into one unit; Charlie was the boss, Ned was his side-kick, Stevie and Spirit were level pegging, and Dom was the baby, so he received the baby treatment, a little bullying but playful nips and gallops included. Ned was the smallest and could be a bit of a bully to all except Charlie: he loved Charlie.

It's funny to witness human-like characteristics in horses. I watched Ned in a particularly grumpy mood. Charlie walked from behind Ned to beside him. Ned swung around and made to chomp Charlie! When Ned realised it was Charlie and not one of the others, the panic in his eyes was priceless. You know the kind of face you'd pull if you'd just realised you'd picked on the wrong person? Well, that was Ned's expression. As for Charlie, I could see him saving that one up for later!

Our boys found other ways to pump up our adrenaline and test our resolve. Our usual routine was to bring them in from the paddock, then tie them to the fence around our cottage. We spread out hay, divided out short-feed most days, and brushed them down.

While munching his hay too quickly, Charlie put his nose on the floor and stayed that way. He remained on his feet, but his eyes blinked in distress. For a few minutes he didn't move. I stroked him, rubbed his neck affectionately, and asked him what was wrong (he didn't reply). But after a few minutes he carried on eating. I thought it was a one-off and didn't think much more about it.

It occurred a few more times. Exactly the same symptoms, then suddenly he'd be okay. He still wouldn't tell me what was going on, and I could see no lasting effects. But, it was Dom that came up with the answer.

As they stood in a line munching their hay, Dom stopped eating. Suddenly he wheezed, a long, screeching, death rasp.

'Untie him, quick!' I didn't know what was happening, but I wanted him away from the fence.

Noel held onto Dom as he continued the wheeze and then stopped. We all stood still for a moment waiting to see what would happen next.

Then Dom stuck his front leg out, stiffened his entire body, and hissed out another agonising wheeze.

'It's okay, boy, steady, steady,' Noel soothed as I checked Dom over.

A few moments later - another gasp.

'Stay here, keep him calm, yell if it gets worse – really yell. I'm calling a vet.'

I bolted into the cottage, banging the doors, and frantically flicked through the phonebook. The second vet practice I rang answered. I explained Dom's symptoms in a frantic breathless monologue.

'He's choking,' the vet said. 'It is a minor choke; he'll be okay.' He explained calmly, 'Get a hose, turn on the water, not too fast, but a good run, put the hose in his mouth – a fair way back, but not so he'll swallow it, but so you make him drink.'

'Right, right,' I said, hopping from one foot to another. 'Can you come if I need you?'

'No, I can't. I'm sorry. This is a minor choke; this should work.' In one movement I replaced the receiver, spun around, and ran for the door. Outside I grabbed the hose and turned the tap on.

'He's still the same,' said Noel, who was noticeably paler.

'He's choking: we need to clear it. Hold him as still as you can,' I yelled as I unravelled the hose, trying not to scare the other horses.

I closed my hand around Dom's chin, below his bottom lip, and lifted his head as high as I could. Without giving him or me time to think, I shoved the hose in his mouth. Noel and I fought to keep him still and steady the hose.

Dom's such a trusting, kind lad; he fidgeted but didn't fight. The water cascaded down my front, down Noel's back, but half flowed into Dom's throat, and I heard a painful swallow.

I pulled out the hose.

The three of us stood together, puffing, dripping, looking at each other. Dom shook his head, then lowered it and started eating the grass, as if nothing had happened.

'Good grief,' Noel said, and that about summed it all up.

11

Jabbing

It was September, and bush fires were raging near Aberdeen on the New England Highway, the town we had planned to start from. These terrifying fires worried me.

'I wouldn't come up this way,' said the BNT coordinator. 'The fire's not reached the track yet, but it's only a few kilometres away; it's set to cross it soon!'

Noel and I unfolded the maps and decided to change our starting point to Taralga, further south of the fires and somewhere that was likely to avoid them altogether. Camping at the town's showground was permitted. Taralga held additional attractions. Clive's cousin, Heidi, lived there with her husband, Ken. It was nice to know that someone we knew of, even if we hadn't met, was nearby.

Our cottage looked like a tack-room *cum* camping-store. We practiced packing up and unpacking. We weighed everything within an inch of its life and marvelled at all the goodies. Waves of excitement swept over me: *Are we really doing this?* I thought. But I didn't have time to dwell; my mind was diverted to the next preparation job on the list. The boys hadn't been jabbed for tetanus before. I wasn't prepared to gamble with a potentially painful death for them.

Tetanus or lockjaw is a serious bacterial infection. The toxin affects the brain and nervous system and can lead to stiffness in the jaw muscles as well as other muscles. The infection causes severe muscle spasms and serious breathing difficulties and can be fatal. I couldn't bear to watch Dom suffering a minor choke!

Our horses hadn't been jabbed, and considering the bush ride we were undertaking, it was now more important than ever.

Andrea wanted Cedar and Jet vaccinated too. Being a nurse, she volunteered to do the first jab and teach us how to inject. They all needed three injections each, with a two week gap between each dose.

We purchased the first seven injections to prevent tetanus and strangles. Strangles is a bacterial infection in the upper respiratory tract of horses that causes enlargement of the lymph nodes in the throat, which could impair breathing. It isn't pleasant and is highly contagious.

Andrea had injected countless people; the closest Noel and I had come to a jab was a sewing needle to prise out a splinter! We searched the internet for advice, discussed tactics, and planned to jab them with the first dose, all in one day.

'Here's your practice equipment.' Smiling mischievously, Andrea handed us each a plump orange. 'Practice with these.' She then gave us a needle each. 'We haven't got a sharps container so, for safety, we'll re-sheath the needle. Always use the one handed technique when re-sheathing so you don't jab your finger.' We were sitting on the grass and Andrea demonstrated the technique by holding the body of the injection equipment while sliding the needle into the protective plastic. The grass kept the plastic sheath still so she could push the needle in, thereby reducing the risk of jabbing her other hand.

This was her first advice; I was nervous already. I felt quite clumsy sometimes, as my hands were usually carrying out the first task on my mind, while my head had leaped forward to the next project. I knew I had to concentrate on one duty at a time with the risky ingredients of a half-a-tonne, fearful animal and a stabbing implement!

Our oranges suffered greatly over the next few days, especially mine. I'd count to three and deftly plunge the needle in, but after a while as I counted, 'One, two,' I'd prod the orange with the needle on each count!

'Brilliant, I'll stab them three times,' I snorted. 'That'll go down well!'

Andrea volunteered to try her boys first. We didn't know what ours would do, but we'd seen Jet react to a needle before. When Andrea and Clive had been away for a while, Jet had suffered a painful abscess in a front foot. I didn't know what was wrong with him but knew something was up when he hadn't moved for two days. I found him in great pain, and feeling responsible, I called out a vet. The abscess was deep, and I didn't see it. The vet was pretty useless, and Jet wouldn't let him stick a needle in his neck. The vet was terrified. Such a fuss was made that I had almost said, 'Give it here, I'll do it!' But I'd not injected before, so I daren't. In the end, we fed Jet antibiotics via powders.

'Okay, Cedar, good boy,' Andrea cooed. Cedar was our first victim; he's a placid boy. Andrea fosters a remarkable connection with her boys. She doesn't have time to ride as much as she'd like, but she's always grooming them, picking off ticks, and scratching their itchy spots; you could see they adored her and the feeling was mutual.

Noel held Cedar, diverting his attention and chatting to him quietly, while I watched Andrea.

'Okay, here's the area we need,' she said drawing an invisible triangle on the main part of Cedar's neck. 'Anywhere in there is fine.' She double checked the contents of the injection and the use-by date. Then, confidently, she slid the needle from its protective sheath, gave Cedar a pat, and put the needle straight in. Swiftly, she pulled the plunger out a little to ensure she hadn't hit a vein and then squeezed in the liquid firmly and pulled the needle out. 'There, that's done.'

'What?' said Noel, spinning around. 'You've done it already? Cedar knew nothing about it, nor did I!'

'The needles are thin,' explained Andrea, modestly ignoring the smooth operation that most certainly was the key.

'Bloody brilliant,' I said, feeling a bit more confident. 'Let's try Jet!'

We ran through the same process. I held Jet this time, so Noel could watch. I chatted to him idly, and suddenly it was done.

'You're a marvel,' Noel said to Andrea. 'If you'd have seen the palaver with the vet and the needle with Jet, you wouldn't believe it!'

Next were our boys.

'Who do you want to do first?' said Andrea calmly, while my tummy started to bubble and pop with anxiety.

We decided on Stevie. Andrea would inject them all today, so we could watch and learn. Within two minutes, he was done – he didn't even blink. Each time Andrea talked us through the process.

Spirit was next, followed by Dom and Charlie. After Stevie, I knew Spirit and Dom would be okay, and they didn't let me down. I was nervous about Charlie; he could be such a wuss.

'There, good boy, Charlie,' said Andrea. 'Nothing to worry about.'

And he was done. Noel and I marvelled at Andrea's deft movements.

Then there was Ned – little Neddy-boy.

I know I didn't help: I was nervous for him. Of course, he sensed this, and a battle ensued. But on the third try, Andrea's tenaciousness won the day. Neddy wriggled and was scared, but we had to push through. He wasn't too impressed, but with a feed with carrots mixed in, Ned soon forgot about his trauma. In two weeks' time we'd inject them all again with Andrea. But for the third and final jab Noel and I would be doing the deed alone.

We had packed the boys up fully twice by this time and ambled out on a couple of short treks. Over-nighters had been undertaken with only part of our equipment. There always seemed to be an adjustment, stitching, shortening, or lengthening to attend to. The injuries and scares had delayed us and eaten into valuable time, but we were ready – sort of.

12

Our First (Or Fifth) Mistake

The night prior to leaving Kangaroo Valley we walked our boys to the front gate and let them into an adjoining paddock. It was about a kilometre from the house to the gate. Cedar and Jet watched as we led them away. Another form of guilt encircled the emotionally-intensive evening; I was taking their mates away. At least they had each other.

Noel and I, and most of the gear, wouldn't fit in the truck; Noel's daughter Mel was following in her car, with us and our gear. The truck would be packed full of horses. Loading our equipment and clearing out the cottage took all afternoon and evening.

Sue and Bill had purchased our car. Sue was planning to commence her trekking adventure in a few months with her friend. They planned to start in Queensland, and Bill would be their support truck. Our car was perfect, hefty on fuel, but with enough grunt to carry lots of gear and power out of trouble. The deal suited us all.

As we were convincing the remaining few bits and pieces into Mel's car, wishing we still had ours, I rolled my right ankle.

'Arrrhhhhh,' I yelled as I my legs folded beneath me. I'd not twisted an ankle before, and I couldn't believe the intense pain.

'For goodness sake,' I sobbed, 'that's all I need!' I sat for a few minutes gathering my breath, calming my anger. I knew the injury would annoy me. Mel strapped me up, and I hobbled around.

'Will you sit down and rest!' Noel said, pausing to view the last few items and ensure I'd received the message. We'd packed up by now, and I was determined to heal overnight.

At dawn the next day, we led the boys into the corral near the gate and bandaged their legs. They ate some hay but were alert to 'something' happening.

'They'll be okay,' Andrea said, resting her hand on my arm in an attempt to quiet my emotions.

I, too, was heavily bandaged and full of pain-killers. Bubbling excitement and dashing adrenaline fought off any lingering pain.

We loaded up Ned first.

'Smallest up front,' our driver said. I'd noticed that Dom had grown taller and longer over the last few weeks. Ned was our smallest. With as much confidence as I could muster, I led him up the ramp; he followed like a lamb. He called to his mates while the partition was closing him in, and the rest followed easily, quickly, all trusting and intrigued with the turn of new events.

I had to walk away from Clive and Andrea when we said farewell. We were only going up the road, but I was so grateful for their love, support, and friendship, my emotions closed my throat, and I choked-up.

Noel, Mel, and I folded ourselves into her car and hauled the last pieces of gear onto our laps. Clive and Andrea pushed closed the doors and waved goodbye. We daren't stop and open a door en route, for mountains of gear and a body would plop out together.

We followed behind the truck, and by 11:30 a.m., we reached Taralga. A clear, bright day welcomed us in. We fell out of the car, dragging equipment that was caught around our legs, and viewed the rich grass and useful corrals. We revelled in having the whole showground to ourselves.

The boys jumped off the back of the truck, snorting at their new surroundings, heads high and keen. It still amazes me that most horses willingly walk up into a truck and allow themselves to be hurtled along at eighty-kilometres an hour, watching the trees flash by.

We tied them up, paid the truck driver, and unpacked Mel's car. While a cup of tea was brewing, Noel's brother, Colin, arrived in his camper van. What a thrill to have family see us off, or to settle us in, for we had to stay a few days to organise our gear and ensure Spirit was one hundred percent okay.

Fortified with tea and biscuits, we tackled the tent. The wind gusted through the grounds and flattened the tent several times. Col left to return home, and we, with the help of Mel, finally pitched the tent.

As with selling all our possessions, saying farewell to family and friends wasn't particularly hard. I'd become emotional leaving Kangaroo Valley and Clive and Andrea, but that was the only time. I was already away from my immediate family in the UK, who follow our escapades with a mix of enthusiasm and anxiety. Our Australian family was still nearby; we weren't going that far. Our friends and families no longer expected us to be static and settle down. During our seventeen years of marriage, we'd always been planning, moving, packing, exploring. The majority of our friends are kept via social media – I'm both appalled and pleased at this thought! How else could we keep in touch leading such vagrant lives? It's one of the bittersweet challenges of travel: disappearing into the ocean or the bush makes the visits and reconnections that much more special. The few close friends we foster are busy with their own adventures; they're always ready to share time, but their lives are like ours, crammed full of living. I constantly (when possible) stay in touch with my family in the UK. I always miss them and long to hear of their lives, but the pull to move and travel is greater – that's just who I am.

With the low voltage electric fence made especially for corralling horses or cattle, we built a temporary paddock opposite the showground where the best grass was tantalisingly free. The horses rolled and played. Then they'd stop to eat for a few minutes. Suddenly Spirit would launch himself straight up in air and gallop off, throwing his head about. We watched him do this twice, chasing the others. There was such glee in his actions; it was a thrill to watch. It brought tears to my eyes witnessing his joy, especially as we'd almost shot him not that long ago.

We rode them every other day, taking care to help build Spirit's muscles. I was positive his leg was back to normal. Ned had a touch of colic one evening, which thankfully disappeared within ten minutes of gentle walking.

All of a sudden, it was time to do the last injection. We thought we'd jab Ned first; we wanted him out of the way. In hindsight, it might have been better to do him last, as we would have been a bit more confident. He was just awful, wriggling and panicking with fearful eyes; his body rigid. But it only took us three attempts. However, once Noel slid the needle into his neck, he didn't pull the plunger back to ensure he wasn't injecting into a vein.

'I couldn't,' he said with his hands on his hips when he'd finished. 'As soon as the needle was in, there was no time – I just had to get it in him!'

I wasn't happy – would he react? What did this mean exactly?

The rest of the boys didn't even know a needle had penetrated their skin, but I was worried about Ned. I rang the help line on the leaflet, and they were fabulous.

'If there's going to be a reaction, it would have happened quickly,' said the vet. 'If he's okay in a few hours, then he'll be fine; just keep an eye on him for a bit, and ring back if he starts sweating for no reason.'

I kept a close eye on Neddy-boy, but he was fine.

The locals of Taralga were the epitome of kindness. The town's journalist interviewed us for the paper, and the owner of the small store was happy to let us sit in her shop with hot coffee and internet for as long as we wanted.

We met Clive's cousin, Heidi, and her husband, Ken. We were invited to dinner, and they quickly became valued friends.

Spirit was back to his old self, and I no longer worried for him. I could see he was ready.

The day we decided to leave, we started packing at 5.30 a.m.; we were ready to leave at 9.30 a.m.

'It's our first 'proper' run,' Noel said. 'We'll get better at it.'

It was exhausting. We didn't dilly-dally either. Their boots went on the front hooves; then the boys that carried the packs had their saddles lifted on; the packs were hauled up last. We didn't want one or two of them standing around for hours with a heavy load. Finally, we checked our campsite one last time, led the boys to the gate, mounted, and headed south.

Taralga is a quiet town, so there weren't many people about. But the store where we purchased feed and the injections was on our route. The staff came out and waved. I am sure they nodded in approval. We looked good loaded up. We had to; there were four hours of work sitting on those horses.

I was behind Noel and his three. I watched the packs carefully, how they sat and moved. My back was tense; I couldn't relax.

Surprisingly, they didn't move or slip; however, I learned a lot about them. How the horses' gait affected the movement, and how high they were. I was still frustrated when we packed up, as lifting the panniers onto the boys was a two-person job. We should have been more independent. But I didn't have the time or confidence to figure out how to do it differently. And I didn't think, I just didn't think. I slipped back into being scared of my own decisions, and this prevented new ideas. The same happened when I started sailing. I closed up and let myself be led by advice. When we started travelling by boat, it was a long time before I gained enough confidence to make decisions and offer new ideas. I had known very little about the nautical world, but once I settled in, the outcome was amazing. I had some marvellous brainwaves, insisting on new rigging, and I created a wonderful and unique tampon/paint idea that I wrote about in my other books.

Here I was again, taking the advice we'd been given and not thinking for myself. It was ridiculous. I didn't have much self-belief at school. I always considered myself not very bright, and I was shy, afraid of revealing my stupidity. I did the same while sailing. I felt so out of my depth and so ignorant, I withdrew into myself. And I was doing it again with the horses. I didn't even realise I was solely following other people's opinions and advice. While most of the information was fantastic and appreciated, I didn't have the wit to think for myself!

So I watched the packs, and I could feel my shoulders rise up towards my ears with the muscles bunching under my tense emotions.

Dom and Stevie's packs were starting to sway. Becoming a maritime skipper (and teacher) had taught me about stability. Top heavy wasn't good. Although their packs weren't top heavy (we kept heavy gear low), they were close to being perilously high. It wouldn't take much to cause a real problem. But I was tired, uptight, and searching for the grass route I thought we'd be riding on by now.

About four kilometres out of camp, we stopped for a wee break and munched on a shared Snickers bar. I'd made some rolls, so Noel and I chewed on them too. The horses tore at the lush grass on the verge beside the road. Excited and nervous butterflies still flitted in our tummies.

The boys dribbled green goo from the rich verge and had a pee themselves. The whole team was feeling comfortable, and while we were hopping back on board, a car pulled up; a pleasant gentlemen chatted with us for a while. He was interested in our journey.

'I live about three kilometres farther along this road,' he said, flicking a glance in the direction we were headed. 'I have plenty of land and a place to rest; please feel free to come in and stay.'

We thanked him but said we'd probably continue on, unless something untoward occurred between then and now. It was our first day, and we wanted to make more miles. It felt like a test, and stopping so soon seemed to be a cop out. It would also mean we'd have spent more time packing the boys than we had travelling! On reflection, we should have just stopped and had an easy day.

We traipsed along, and the boys settled down and strode out happily. They enjoyed the novel surroundings, especially Charlie, who had to look at everything new as if it had been laid out especially for him.

I heard a truck rumbling towards us, and my back muscles bunched. Horses sense every move you make. Even Ned, I knew, would sense my firmer grip on the end of his lead rope. Noel's three didn't worry, but Charlie tensed beneath me. The space was tight, and the truck didn't slow. Ned's eyes bulged when he spotted the truck. My legs and hands shifted into automatic drive, pushing Charlie over. As the vehicle thundered towards Ned, he dug his hooves into the soft soil. As he pulled, he pivoted. My habitual steering of Charlie was still functioning. But Ned was powerful, I wouldn't let go, and the chaffing sensation on the soft part of the top of my hand, between my thumb and finger, spelled out the start of a worrisome wound. Slowly the rope ground its way along and ripped a good chunk of skin off. But I hung on tighter as Ned fought. Although it felt like minutes, in just a few seconds the truck was gone. Ned sighed, relaxed, and carried on. My eyes were watering, my hand bleeding and stinging with a fierce throb that zapped through my nerves. But Ned was okay.

Noel hadn't seen what happened; his boys walked along merrily, without a care. Later I showed him my burn.

'Gloves for you!' he said. 'And how's that blasted ankle?'

My ankle was better, sore but bandaged. I could manage.

Drinking Cow Poo

How hard could a twenty-kilometre trek be? Terribly, achingly, horrifyingly hard. After packing up for several hours, we were exhausted before we started. The boys were fresh and eager. But there was road, road, and more blasted road!

I am embarrassed to reveal that my research was less than adequate. I claim full responsibility for the assumption we'd be on grass. What sounds like a minor hiccup led to a snow-balling effect of worries.

The road continued, and my dream of plodding along bouncy trails, surrounded by Australian bush, was shattered. We couldn't get off the road. Cars roared past. I'd yell at those who skimmed my leg – didn't they realise a horse can side-step in a second without forewarning?

The boys wore no shoes, only boots on their front, load-bearing feet. We'd researched the 'right' way to do this and had decided to try bare-foot. Our bare-foot farrier agreed that the back hooves would be fine. But we all based this assessment on riding off tar road; now we were doing road work, and their feet were suffering.

As the hours plodded by, the boys tried to climb up on banks; I knew their feet were sore. The advice from the pack-saddle seminar came back to haunt me.

'I will never go packing in company with others that do not have shoes on,' Julia had said. 'My companion's horses' feet were terrible.' Julia was a long-term packer; she ventured out for weeks at a time. One of her companions had a horse with bare feet; the horse had suffered. I remembered her words, but at the time the significance didn't sink in. I'd actually thought she said that horses 'with' shoes were the problem. There was so much to absorb, take in, and write down. It was disappointing and pivotal that I didn't distil that particular crystal of wisdom. We would all pay for it.

Our boys were not comfortable, but at least the tarmac road was turning into a muddy passageway. No more cars, but it was stony! I whimpered – I don't know why – for the pain I was causing our boys, for my stupidity. Fortunately, a wider verge emerged, and we traipsed through soft grass.

'They all need four boots,' I said to Noel, glancing worriedly towards the stony track. 'We can't expect to do this again. How much road is there, do you think?'

'I don't know,' he replied. 'I had assumed it would be mostly dirt.'

And that was our mistake, a stupid, stupid mistake. The 'trail' was mostly tarred road!

As we approached the camp, my burn was smarting and needing attention, Noel's knees were aching, my ankle was throbbing, and we both had sore bottoms. We couldn't wait to dismount. The whole team was in pain, one way or another, and we were hating it!

The responsibility weighed heavy on my shoulders. Both Noel and I had aches from past injuries and current (silly) ideas. Noel's knees always suffered. Motorbike riding for years had left them 'thin.' The cold seeped in rapidly and caused them to ache without much encouragement. My sprained ankle was taking its time healing.

We'd traversed 20.5 kilometres. That's a fair amount in one day. We were walking at a speed of around three kilometres per hour. That's about six hours riding. Plus stops to chat to passers-by (many were interested in five packed-up horses), wee stops, pack-adjustment delays, traffic, and map reading.

We spied our next camp. Well, it was a location that had grass and a fence on three sides, but no water. To the right we spotted a dam in the neighbouring field.

Dismounting became a challenge. After six hours in the saddle, we were molded into position. Convincing our limbs to react as if we were in our twenties and land with a spring was not a laughing joke, more a whimpering, slightly hysterical giggle.

The physical pain matched the emotional in intensity. Then two miracles occurred. I spotted the land owner's name and phone number posted on a sign on the gate that gave access to the watering hole, and we had mobile reception. I dialled the number, waiting for a flat battery or an answering machine. However, a cheery voice answered and was glad to permit us access for water. Defeating one problem fuelled my energy reserves for the next. But water first.

We unloaded the boys and led them through the cows and down the hill to the water. They were alert but relaxed, hoping, no doubt, we'd let them go in this giant field, so they could scarper and act the fool. Their loose lips hung in the cool water, sucking up the muddy liquid and dirt. Grateful swallows punctured the silence until Dom created his own music. He lifted his strong leg, threw it forward, and let it fall into the water, pawing, splashing, and loving every minute. As I watched his legs begin to fold beneath him, I tugged on his lead rope.

'No, Dom,' I said, while keeping the line taut. 'You are not rolling in that!'

Noel and I stooped down to fill our drinking bottles and shower bags. One square bag was enough for us both to shower, the other for the 'kitchen' and washing hands. Our drinking water was scooped into silver stainless bottles. The watering hole had plenty of 'bits' in it. When it was hot, the cows stood in the cool water, and at some point they'd have to poo. I tried not to think about this too much. We'd made a decision that if the boys drank the water, we did too. We did boil it first, though.

Back at camp, we released the boys. They roamed and hid within the trees, with plenty to eat. With only one side to block off where the grassy trail met the dirt track, we swiftly constructed the fence and pitched our tent just inside the corral.

What we hadn't envisaged or planned for was the setting up of our camp. We knew we had to set up our base, but after ensuring the horses were fed, watered, safe, and happy, it was a good hour or two before we could start ensuring we were fed, watered, safe, and happy. Just moving all the gear that the boys carried all day to the eaves of the tent, or under canvas, was a massive job. There was so much. I also wanted to sort out the boots for the boys.

Fortunately, with plenty of battery power on the mobile, I rang the boot people. With a lot of guessing, some support, and little fretting and lots of relief, we ordered boots. We'd take delivery at Crookwell Post Office, our next stop. They weren't cheap, but I didn't care; my concern for their welfare seemed to over-shadow everything. Later on I'd realise that Noel and I needed some of my concern too, not just five strong, healthy horses!

In the evening, we wandered along the grass to ensure they hadn't broken loose into another paddock. They were content, munching the short thick grass. A neighbouring mare and her foal galloped over to say hello. Our boys were polite but not that interested; they had each other and lots of food. They'd worked hard all day and were hungry. The foal hung around, and mum left. After a while the foal understood that there was no playtime here and thundered off back to mum.

As dark crept up on us, I hoped I could stay awake long enough to witness the night time theatre I'd been promised. Noel's brother had told me that in the bush the 'stars can be so bright you think you can stretch up and touch them.' But lifting my tea to my cracked lips was becoming an effort, both my limb and the mug's combined weight making it heavy work, so we shuffled into our tent and gratefully slid into our sleeping bags. We'd survived our first day; a mostly successful day, a safe camp, a warm dry bed, and five reasonably happy horses: what more could a girl wish for?

'Crunch, munch, crunch, munch.'

'What the...?' I woke with a start.

'Bugger off,' yelled Noel. 'Go on, bugger off!'

We lay quietly. Then, TWANG, trip, stagger, thud! The tent shook.

'For goodness sake, why do they want the grass under the tent?' Noel seethed as we pulled on our jeans.

The boys were around the tent, between the guy ropes, and pushing their noses under the canvas. One tripped and almost fell on us! We shooed them away, but they were reluctant to go. As we moved the fence, they started behaving like naughty children. At eleven o'clock at night, when we were tired, we spoke some harsh words but got the job done and fenced them away from the tent.

Back in bed I realised I hadn't taken the chance to look at the night sky. Sighing, I closed my eyes and tried not to dwell on how tough the first day had been, and how ridiculously under-prepared we were.

In the morning, Dom was a little way from the others, and I stepped through the long grass towards him, my feet entangling in the mature pasture. An old, solid, split-rail fence lay hidden on its side in the grass. The gaps between the rails were just wide enough for a hoof and just deep enough to break a leg if it caught and panic ensued. With my heart thumping, I skipped across the fence before Dom could move. He liked to play, and I didn't want him trotting over this fence. I caught him and found a safe part to traverse and thanked my lucky stars there were no injuries.

Noel and I walked the horses down the neighbouring paddock for another drink. Dom splashed and tried to roll. He was so sweet and good natured and sought fun in everything he did, as if he was saying, *Come on, let's play!* But we wanted to move on.

Another few hours of packing, and we were on our way. Along this section we found plenty of verges with soft grass to protect the horses' bare feet.

The next camp was fourteen kilometres away. The roads were smooth dirt, and there were plenty of good grass verges – a big relief for us all. The route narrowed, but we still met the odd car. We were in our usual format, Noel on Stevie with Spirit tied to the back of his saddle and Dom tied to Spirit. I was on Charlie leading Ned by hand.

We would have liked to stop at the small Travelling Stock Reserve (TSR) at Rosslyn, but the 'water availability' that our guidebook promised via a private home was not supported. When we rang the number in our guidebook, they 'ummed' and 'ahhed,' and we realised they weren't interested.

'They should just make it clear they don't want to help!' I said, exasperated.

However, in Rosslyn there was a fire station. No one was there, but there was a tap.

'I'll dig out the canvas bucket from my saddle-bags,' I said, as I rummaged in the pockets.

'Good, I need to get off,' Noel said with a groan as he slid to the ground.

We took it in turns to hold the five reins and fill the bucket; they all slurped up mouthfuls of water, us too. We continued along wide verges with good feed and good travelling, I tried not to think too much about lurking snakes!

'The TSR should be here somewhere.' Noel dropped Stevie's reins as he checked the map that lay on Stevie's shoulder in a watertight, see-through envelope. As we sank into a dip in the road, we could see the paddock on our right, falling away from us. We led the horses into an enormous field where we could see no end and proceeded to argue. It just wasn't "us" to argue. It was from exhaustion, the unknown, and, more so, from fear.

Our argument was about the paddock we pegged out. We both had different ideas. The ridiculous thing was we were talking just a few metres difference. Every 'greener' bit of grass, I wanted and needed to include into the boys' paddock. This meant a few odd shapes and a bit of jiggery-pokery up the side of a hill. I was overwhelmed with a need to do the best I could for them, even if it meant totally ignoring the fact that we were tired and had to find water, make camp, and eat our first substantial meal (probably a mug of soup) of the day.

'Don't put that post there!' I called over to Noel. 'I want it further up the bank.'

Noel sighed and yanked out the spiked plastic pole he'd just banged into the ground.

'No, not there, can't you see the greener grass right there?' I pointed.

'There's enough grass here for the night: why make everything such hard work?'

'They need good food. I can't rest unless I know I've done the best I can for them. Move that pole, please.' I'd asked nicely but my words were still strained.

'Do it yourself; I am exhausted.' And with that Noel stomped off back to our gear, and I finished pegging out the corral.

With a cup of miso soup filling our empty stomachs, Noel and I sat together, talking as if the row hadn't happened. We had been stupid and tired. Our energy was zapped dry.

In the dwindling light, we followed the creek west to deeper and cleaner water to fill the shower bags. The cold water made our skin taut and bumpy.

'No squealing,' I said to Noel, vigorously rubbing the goose-bumps away after my shower. We laughed, naked in the middle of the paddock. The shower washed away the day and all bad feelings.

The horses' corral was low set, and they were uncomfortable. When spooked, horses run to high ground, they like to see the enemy approach. When a kangaroo appeared at dusk at the peak of the hill, our boys galloped around nervously.

'Good grief, what on earth are they going to do when they see twenty?' I said, searching the horizon for more. They'd only glimpsed one kangaroo at this point.

'They can't have seen them before.' Noel joined me in scanning the horizon. 'They must have gone from the paddock to the racetrack and back.'

'You're right,' I said. 'It's a good point; it shows, too, when Charlie walks around looking at his surroundings as if he hadn't realised there were other parts to his world!'

The next day we decided to move on; we should have stopped and rested. We were tired and niggly with each other. This behaviour was not usual for us; Noel and I are great mates, and the thought that we had become this way made us both miserable. Short words punctuated with long sighs flowed between us as we prepared for the day with the boys tied up halfway between our camp and their paddock. We were out of our comfort zone, and this was affecting our behaviour. Silently we both seemed to decide to just shut up: neither of us could say anything nice, so we said nothing, mutually understanding it was the situation not the relationship that was changing our personalities. Over time we have developed strong characters. When Noel and I first met, we were both a little lost. I was twenty-six and had just lost my fiancé; Noel was forty-four and walking away from a long-term relationship. Not only did our desires to be free make us click, but we had the necessary foundations, ideas, and support to nurse each other through the tough times that ending relationships, for whatever reason, brought. Together we bolstered each other's flagging morale and self-appreciation. Noel saved my life during my darkest times, and he still keeps me on my toes. Not only does my life have to challenge me, so does my partner; Noel hasn't let me down (or off the hook!) once.

At the end of the packing, we had two stainless steel hooks left over; they were superfluous. We left them on a round fence post, thinking someone would find a use for them.

Finally, we were on our way, with more road work to do. The road was quiet, but when traffic appeared it raced past. On our left was a paddock lined with trees fighting for space. I spotted a small kangaroo hopping between the trunks. I knew it would jump out at us. I don't know why, but I knew. And it did. Straight out, directly toward the boys, as if it had read my mind. The troop took off en masse. Charlie and Ned galloped together. Neddy hadn't seen what the panic was about, but Charlie took off so Ned did too! We galloped three hundred metres up the road before I could stop them both. Behind I could hear Noel.

'No, stop, what the...? No, NO, for goodness sake. Nooooo!'

He had pulled Stevie to a halt straight away, but the others had tried to continue on. He hopped off Stevie, but Spirit and Dom were intent on knitting themselves together, good and tight.

'Steady, steady, stand, STAND!' Noel repeated until they finally stopped moving. As I made my way back to Noel and his bundle of horses and rope, I couldn't work out if they had stopped because of our marvellous training ('stand') or because they couldn't move. As I approached, I realised it was the latter.

Noel and his string of three had bound themselves into a rather tight pretzel, right in the middle of the road. We scooted them sideways – they hopped, skipped, and jumped in the direction we pushed them. I noted that not all legs reached the floor! The boys looked like they had been playing cats-cradle, but they stood still while we untangled them. They were coming down off their adrenaline trip and were calm. They allowed us to man-handle them and release their binds. It was a great form of trust; they watched us, knowing we'd sort them out. They were all blowing hard, and our adrenaline was still galloping, but there were no injuries.

Of course the packs needed re-adjusting. After an hour of undoing knots and straightening bags out, we squared our shoulders and set off once again. It was about 10 a.m., and already heavy fatigue pulled at our limbs.

It was on this part of the journey that we introduced the boys to more new tests. As we strode along, Charlie suddenly darted across to the other side of the road. Ned kept in step with him.

'What are you doing, Charlie?' I asked, as if he'd answer me. 'You can't just fly across the road like that!' My legs and arms were working in unison, guiding Charlie back to the left side of the road. For a moment, I couldn't understand what had inspired this odd manoeuvre, until we reached more painted lines in the road. Charlie was scared of them, but I was ready. The white-painted road sign obviously made him wary. With firm hands and legs, I made him walk over the road markings, and with a hop to spring over them, he realised then they weren't going to hurt him. He sighed and strolled on.

We all plodded along merrily until Charlie suddenly arced his body away from a mail box. He kept his head pointed at it, so he could keep an eye on the strange structure and make sure it didn't leap at him. He didn't like letterboxes either! After a few dozen, he relaxed a bit, but he still kept a good eye on them.

Despite Charlie's oddities, we had a good day beating a path to Crookwell, but we were in the teeth of the wind, and Charlie started to irritate me. He insisted on walking right up the backsides of Noel's group. I tried to pull him back about ten paces and keep him there, but he wouldn't have it. There was safety within a tight group, and with the wind and Ned and his nervous ways, they were like steam trains. I gave up in the end, and our tight bunch huddled together all the way.

As we approached Crookwell, the grass and trees gave way to houses and traffic again. It was quiet, and we turned off the main road before we reached the town centre and climbed a hill to the glorious showground.

'Hello, are you going to the showground?' A friendly chap stopped his car to ask our intentions.

'Yes, if that's okay?' I asked.

'Sure is, I'm the manager. I'll be back in a few minutes to show you where to go.'

'Great, thanks!'

We tied the boys up to a convenient post near the main entrance and tried to figure out what to do next. We wanted to relieve them of their load as soon as possible, but the showground stretched over several kilometres, and we didn't know where we'd be camping. We waited impatiently.

'I'm taking their gear off,' Noel muttered as he loosened Spirit's straps. I agreed and made my way to Ned to unload his bags. Of course, halfway through the unpacking process the manager arrived and pointed to the other side of the showground.

Actually, he gave us the run of the whole place and said, 'As long as you are out of here by February, then all will be well!'

We made camp under a shelter (no walls, just a roof). The boys mowed through wonderful grass and had a shelter if they were brave enough to venture into it (it was dark). The open golf course that butted up to their paddock meant they felt secure; they could see for miles.

We decided to stay a few days. A low-frontal weather system was forecast to bring rain and wind. We rugged up the horses at night and purchased extra hay, which they turned their noses up at. It was rather coarse, but I figured that they couldn't be that hungry.

They galloped around their little paddock at 3 a.m., when hail came and clattered down on the tin roof. However, they stayed in their corral, safe in the company of each other. During the day, we watched as one by one, they lay down together – we weren't the only ones who were beat.

The new boots arrived, and all fitted except Stevie's. He had square feet, so we returned his boots and ordered from a different supplier.

The boys thought nothing of having four boots on, except Neddy. He was excellent with his feet. He always tried to help. When you asked him to pick up a leg, he'd whip it up so sharply it was almost dangerous. But this was Neddy's way of helping. All he wanted to do was please us.

We put a boot on his back leg, and he became a little wide-eyed. Then he kicked back his leg in a comical frantic spurt, until the boot flew off!

He wasn't nervous, but it was something new, and that always made him tense. So we took our time. I held up Ned's leg and slid the boot over his hoof. As I began to release his leg, Noel whipped up his other back leg, so he had to stand in the boot. He offered a few kicks, the boots didn't move, so he gave a 'Neddy-shrug' and soon forgot all about them.

'The wind's picking up; we'll need to tie down the tent.' Noel proceeded to utilise his nautical knot-knowledge to hold our home in place. We weren't worried about the rain as we had the extra shelter under the roof.

To gain relief from the wind, we sat in the tent and read. When I had ridden as a kid, I suffered with painful leg cramps. Twenty-or-so years later, it was making a return appearance with zeal. Climbing in and out of the tent required crouching, which was a prime recipe for cramp. When the cramps reached my thighs, it was as if someone was tearing my muscles in two. It was enough to make me yell out in agony.

It was during this windy afternoon when I heard someone call out, 'Is there anyone there?'

I said, 'Yes, hang on,' and tried to undo the tent zip while kneeling down. The zip caught, my leg cramped, and I had to lie down quickly and push out my leg immediately. As I flung myself on the floor, my head popped out of the small opening I had made running the zip up. Unfortunately, beside the zip was half a bottle of wine, so as my head plopped out, the wine bottle was knocked over and rolled towards our visitor. I yelped, 'arrrhhhhhhhhhhhhhhhhhh, grab my toes, grab my toes, quick, grab my toes!' The cramp had taken hold, and I needed Noel to bend my toes back to pull against the muscle.

With my head outside the tent, my body inside, and the wine bottle at our visitor's feet, I breathed a sigh of relief. 'Ahhh that's better.'

With an amused expression, Noel watched my mad antics, pulled back my toes, and then leisurely clambered out of his side of the tent to meet a somewhat scared-looking visitor. 'Erm, hello,' he said tentatively, a startled look on his face. 'Is she okay?"

'Yes, she's fine, does this all the time,' Noel replied with a grin.

'I saw you at the TSR, and I think you left something behind.' He held up our metal hooks, the ones we'd left on the gate post.

'Can you use them?' said Noel. 'We don't need them any longer; we thought finders would be keepers.'

'Well, yes, probably,' he said, peering at them in his hand.

'They're yours then.'

14

The Art of Conversation

'We have too much gear,' Noel said.

I nodded my agreement while he continued.

'How about we go through every single item, one at a time, and discard what we can manage without?'

'Good idea,' I said, starting to haul the gear from each bag.

We dispensed with ten kilograms of gear: folding stools, farrier apron, spare clips, extra jumpers, and so on.

A fortuitous meeting with a local family, who rode in the showground to exercise their horses, meant we had someone to take the gear. The wife's sister lived near Noel's daughter and had offered to drop it all back to Mel. Sadly, when we returned home, our horse gear was significantly lighter than ten kilograms!

The rains came, and our tent leaked, not from the top, but somehow from the bottom, and we woke up with a minor lake under our mattresses. Sodden, cold, and tired, we emptied the tent and lashed it up high under the shelter to dry it out. The showground manager took pity on us and opened up a large hall *cum* shed.

'You can camp in there if you like,' he said pointing into the cavernous space that stored tables and chairs.

Pure luxury for us!

We walked into town most days and soon became 'known.' Either that or it was the scruffy, dirty clothes and un-brushed hair that made people look at us.

Walking back to the showground one afternoon, Noel accidently scratched his face, and it bled. As a few droplets ran down his cheek, passers-by gave us funny looks.

'We're not dangerous!' said Noel to one couple. Meanwhile I was too busy giggling. I rather needed a pee at that moment, which sent me into more fits of giggles. I looked drunk; Noel looked beaten up. This was a strange existence.

Having sailed together for years, living on a small boat, Noel and I had become best buddies. We do everything together and have a great understanding of each other's moods, emotions, wants, and needs. Noel's taught me to laugh at myself, and not many days pass without us both clutching our stomachs in fitful giggles, usually at something one of us has done or said. Whether we are trekking on a trail or bobbing in oceans or walking along the street, we find humour in most situations – life's too short to be serious too often. There just isn't enough time; why not laugh through the limited time we have? I try to live by this philosophy, but it isn't always possible.

Leanne was the trail's co-ordinator for this section, and she was a great support. Her aunt, Beatrice, lived in Crookwell, and while Leanne was busy working, her aunt came to see if we were okay. Beatrice invited us to join her and her friends at the RSL (Returning Serviceman's League) for dinner on Friday. We readily agreed.

Beatrice was delightful company and highly respected throughout the town. The club was a typical Australian country club. Nothing fancy, in fact the inside hadn't seen a coat of paint for quite some time. But it didn't matter. The atmosphere was friendly and inviting. We sat with our host and her friends and took great pleasure in soft chairs and interesting conversation.

For dinner we both ordered enormous T-bone steaks, which we consumed in about ten minutes. It was the best meal I'd ever had.

The bar was an adventure in itself. Ordering at this saloon was a bit of an experience. I wandered up to the square, dark-timbered bar. The blonde lady at the till flicked her head upwards slightly, as if indicating, *what d'ya want?*

'Could I see the wine list please?'

Her response was a simple, but effective *snort!*

'Erm, what wine do you have then?'

'Chardonnay,' she said, her response accompanied by rolling eyes.

I waited for a moment, but that seemed to be the complete list. The bar-lady picked up the cardboard box as if to prove she had Chardonnay and held it in the air to speed my decision. As I hesitated, she jutted out her left hip and expelled a sigh that clearly asked, *do you want it or not?*

'Thanks, a Chardonnay will be fine.' I smiled, feeling quite out of place.

I ordered a beer for Noel and handed over a ten dollar note, for I was not privileged enough for her to divulge the cost. I held my hand out for the change and realised that throughout the entire order the only word the bar-lady had said was *Chardonnay*!

We enjoyed our stay at Crookwell; it's a place with lots of community spirit. Paul, the showground's manager, had built up the grounds with the help of a formidable team. The showground is privately owned and run by the town-folk – it's rather a splendid ground, too, and a place the locals are proud of, and rightly so. We were comfortable there; it didn't seem to matter if we were smart or scruffy, clever or just 'run of the mill'; everyone was welcoming and friendly.

We were well-rested, and it was time to go. We climbed the short hill to the showground gates, reluctant to leave. But the boys were marching on, ready to explore.

For the first two hours I watched the packs. Along this section, we'd traverse a busy road for about twenty minutes. My mouth was dry. Mammoth, rattling trucks hurried by, and I had to concentrate to relax and not let my emotions flow through to Charlie and Ned. I blew a sigh of relief when I spotted the wide grass verges skirting the dual carriageway. The truck drivers slowed down and gave us plenty of room.

We stopped for a wee break. Charlie started fidgeting. Ned was still weeing. Noel was standing right next to the barbed wire fence with his three, and I was a short way in front. Charlie forced his strong head down to loosen the reins from my hands and walked off in the direction of the others.

'Charlie.... no, Ned's trying to...' Poor Ned held still as long as he could before he was dragged mid-wee with me and Charlie: I couldn't let him go. By this time, Charlie had spun around, and he suddenly took off. He galloped the few, short strides to Noel's group. When we became trapped in a corner between Noel and the fence, Charlie dipped his shoulder and did a one hundred and eighty degree turn that defied his bulk. This launched me straight out of the saddle and into the fence. All of a sudden I was sitting on the ground with my legs under the barbed wire. My leg narrowly avoided being cut on the wire, but a crippling cramp shot through it.

'Ahhh,' I yelled, grabbing my leg.

'Are you okay? What is it?' Noel jumped off and stood next to me, his eyes scrunched in concern.

'I'm okay, I'm okay,' I said breathlessly. 'It's just cramp!' I rubbed my leg, trying to convince the contracting muscle to let go.

Noel grabbed Ned, who was happy to stay with the group. Charlie, however, thought it was time to go adventuring on his own and took off up the middle of the main road.

I jumped up and ran after him. I was trying not to appear as if I was chasing him, but I had to go fast enough to catch him up. It was like a B-grade movie. Every time Charlie swung his head around to look at me, I slowed down and pretended I wasn't there.

When he looked forward, I ran to catch him up. He was half-having fun and half-scared of being told off. He was revelling in his freedom though.

Meanwhile, the traffic had stopped. Large, bulky trucks halted in both directions, and as I trotted past one, I heard the driver call out on his radio, 'There's a woman down and a horse loose!' Embarrassed, I waved my thanks as I continued to pursue Charlie.

I was thankful that the truck drivers gave us so much time and space.

I eventually caught Charlie. 'It's okay, good boy, come on,' I said to him, giving him a gentle pat. His furtive glances spoke volumes; he was wondering about my reaction.

We walked back to the rest of the group. 'What was all that about?' asked Noel.

'I have no idea.' I shrugged. 'Something set him off.'

We mounted up and continued on. The large lorries were extra cautious, and soon we gratefully turned off onto a laneway.

I was in front for a while when Noel figured out what had upset Charlie. 'It's his tail: underneath it is all red,' he said, encouraging Stevie forward so he could take a closer look. 'Maybe the lead rope became caught under it; it looks a bit like a burn.'

'That'd do it, if only he'd stop instead of running off!'

'It doesn't look too bad,' continued Noel. 'And he doesn't seem worried by it. We can have a look later.'

'That'll be fun,' I murmured. Charlie could be a bit snobbish about his privates.

Along the laneway, we checked the maps and turned our heads away from the driving, freezing, stinging rain that had decided to accompany us.

'It's only a few more kilometres,' Noel said. 'And the weather's improving.' As he spoke these words into the wind, it ceased blowing, and the rain stopped. The clouds cleared, and suddenly the day became pleasant.

A car stopped beside us, and a young chap stuck his head out of the window.

'Take care, there are plenty of trucks coming this way tomorrow. We're mining nearby.'

'Thanks for the warning; we may sit-tight tomorrow, maybe leave the following day,' Noel explained.

'I'll let the drivers know.'

'Thanks, that's kind of you; the drivers have been fantastic, slowing down and taking care. If you speak to them, do pass on our thanks,' I said with a grin.

'That's nice to know; I certainly will,' he replied, and drove off with a friendly wave.

It's moments like these that restore your faith in humanity.

The TSR stretched up to our left in the form of two fenced paddocks carpeted with thick, tasty grass and furnished with a large dam. We led our boys in and found a flat spot for our campsite, unloading as close as we could.

We all ambled down to the other end of the ten acre paddock, to show the boys the water and to have a bit of a scout about. The long grass would surely be hiding a few snakes, though I tried to put that thought out of my head.

The boys sucked up the cool water and inspected their surroundings. The hill stretched up towards where we would camp; surrounding the paddock was a patchwork of other fields, a horse's dream. We let the boys go.

We made camp, and for once it built up smoothly and didn't seem arduous. By now the sun was shining. It was a beautiful spot. Tall trees reached up into the endless blue. Rich greens surrounded the vista, with the odd house scattered on neighbouring hills for company, but with our privacy still intact.

The boys loved this paddock; they jumped in the water, rolled in it, pawed at it and splashed. They galloped, bucked, and ran amok, having a great time.

I was grateful to slip into my comfy bed, but I was all too aware I was running out of sleeping positions. I could no longer sleep on my back, for my back ached after ten minutes. Not once have I been able to sleep on my front. I could sleep on my right thigh only; my left was purple and blue from my fall earlier. I still fell into a deep sleep.

The following day, Noel and I found logs to sit on, and we carried out repairs. It was here we received the first review of our recently published book, *Cruisers' AA (accumulated acumen)*. Our wealth of knowledge of sailing and cruising had been poured into this book, and a sailing magazine had done a write-up. Noel's brother had downloaded the review and texted us snippets.

'It's all positive!' I grinned at Noel. 'Actually, it's great!'

'Fantastic,' he beamed. 'I can't believe we're sitting in the middle of a paddock reading a review of the book!'

We opened up the second paddock for the boys and built the electric fence around our campsite to keep them out. Charlie still wandered over as close as he could to watch me carefully while I took a shower.

'Go away, you perv!' I laughed at him. I wasn't sure what his voyeuristic expectations were.

Noel and I sat companionably together, sewing tears, oiling leather, and hand-washing clothes.

Snort.

'What was that?' I asked as I jumped.

Behind us was another paddock with trees lining the fence. Between the trees, the head of a massive bull poked through. He snorted and pawed the ground.

'Oh, he likes you!' I smirked.

The bull moved forward, snorted more, then started to dribble; he grunted in a rather ugly way.

'Have you figured out your escape route?' I asked Noel. 'That fence will slow him down for about two and a half seconds at most.' I had already worked out which tree I could climb, should the bull choose to join us. But he didn't; he just liked being nearby.

We stayed for two nights; we should have stayed longer. It was the perfect place, and the boys enjoyed it immensely, cavorting and bucking. They put on a little weight, and the gloss in their coats started to gleam.

We left the following day and trekked along more lane-ways until the country road gave way to another, wider road. The route to Gurrandah was quiet and offered a glorious vista of vast paddocks, some with new wind farms.

15

Bruised Boy

About two-thirds of the way to Gurrandah TSR, Noel experienced some difficulties. Spirit became irritable with Dom. I thought Dom was tired and pulling back on Spirit. I tried to gee him on, and for a while they settled down. Soon, Dom started dragging back again, and Spirit pulled his ears back, their tips pointing to his tail in anger.

'Give me Spirit for a bit,' I said, reaching for the lead rein. 'See if that helps.' Noel sighed and handed him over. I led Spirit with Ned for a while, but it was hard with three abreast on a busy road. I tried to push Ned and Spirit behind Charlie.

'Give him back here; it's too dangerous that way.'

Spirit obediently changed positions again. I imagined him sighing, *Make up your mind.*

Then Dom fell down. All of a sudden he was on his knees. Such are their head collars, the lead rope caused the nose strap to close over his nostrils, preventing full breath, and struggling to suck in a lung full of air, he hopped back up. We checked his pack: everything seemed to be in order. I just didn't know what to do. I considered unloading him and hiding the gear in the bush and asking someone to collect it later, by car. But we were on another main road – there was nowhere to do it. Our next stop was a TSR; there would be no one around. We pushed on.

Was he tired? He still had a bounce in his step.

Is he being naughty? He just isn't naughty, not that kind of naughty – cheeky yes, but not badly behaved.

Dom put his nose on the ground and left it there while he walked. I knew there was a problem. My shoulders bunched up beneath my neck in concern. Dom pushed on and appeared comfortable with his head down – Spirit calmed, and we carried on. Not long after, we found our camp. A fenced paddock with little grass and water, but it was heaven as we could stop, and I could unwind my shoulders and see to Dom.

We unloaded the boys, and beneath Dom's saddle there were no marks. He trotted off to reach the others, happy, appearing injury free. They sourced the best grass, and a little later we led them to the water and checked the fences. The TSRs are not used often, so mending and moving loose wire and ensuring they were safe was a job that had to be done. We knew we'd have to ferry more water over from the creek across the fence too – there wasn't enough in the paddock.

While sorting through our gear, Leanne, the BNT coordinator for this section, drove up to our camp. She brought us sausages and steak – the mere thought of eating them filled my mouth with saliva. I talked to her about Dom, who was hiding some way off.

'He's young; he's probably just acting the fool,' she said. But I had my doubts: he wasn't playing; he was trying to get comfortable. It was late, and as there was such sparse grass, we decided to stay just one night.

As a rule we brushed them down before loading up. Going over their bodies with a soft brush kept them healthy, but primarily it was to comb-off dried sweat and check for injuries, lumps and bumps, before we loaded them up.

The next day as I was working on Dom, I found the problem. As I ran the brush over his shoulders his skin twitched violently. I placed the brush on a fence post and ran my hands over the top of his withers. He twitched again, but he didn't put his ears back. I pressed harder, and his legs buckled.

'I've found out what the problem was with Dom.' I called to Noel as he busied himself with Stevie and Spirit. 'We've bruised

Dom's back.' With that I burst into tears. How could I? This beautiful boy did everything we asked, and look what we did to him!

We checked the set up and discovered that when we had tied extra cord on each side of his pack-saddle to keep it together, we'd obviously done it up too tight and pinched him.

'He'll be okay,' Noel soothed.

'I'm supposed to know what I am doing,' I sobbed. 'I'm responsible for these animals, and I can't even stop them becoming injured.' I was forlorn.

'Do you have a bruise?' Noel asked.

'What?' I sniffed, unsuccessfully searching for a tissue.

'You have bruises, don't you? Show me your hand.' Noel peered at my wound. 'Ned caused the burn on your hand; you still ride, even though it's painful, right?'

I looked at the injury and ran my calloused hands over my bruises at various and numerous locations.

'These boys are tough. It's just bruising; he doesn't blame you – he was just uncomfortable. Now let's figure out what to do.'

I sighed a Ned-like sigh and tried to rein in my emotions.

'Well, we can't saddle him up – I can't even ride him. We have too much gear to leave him bare-back.'

'How long will it take to heal?'

I checked Dom's back again, I could feel two long, warm lumps on either side of his withers. With a soft stroke he flinched.

'Two to three weeks, I think.'

Noel was taken aback. 'It may be sooner, but I'd say we'd be lucky to have him completely healed in ten days. It's pretty severe bruising, and carrying gear all day...' I trailed off. However, I am not a vet, and as I'd been out of the game for some time, I was guessing.

Luckily, there were bars of signal on the phone, and with some help from the internet, we found a woman with a horse truck, heading our way - on the return journey from another job.

'Yes, you'll all fit, and the gear. I'll be there around twelve.'

We arranged a drop-off at Hall Showground, stopping at a bank on the way.

Leap-frogging this section of the trail was fine. In two more days we would have reached a chronically busy section of the BNT that the guidebooks recommended trucking past anyway.

The next BNT coordinator, from Hall, confirmed that we could camp at the showground with no problem. He telephoned a few times, as he knew we were having difficulties. The support was welcomed.

Blessed with the transport arriving in just a few hours, we organised our gear and ferried it all to the bottom of the hill, nearer the road, via Stevie and Spirit. We piled it up, collected the rest of the herd, and waited, letting them munch the long verge grass. Bang on time, our rescuer emerged.

We loaded the gear, the boys ran up the ramp, and we were off. Relief flooded through my aching limbs. At the next stop we could rest, call a vet, re-group, and decide what to do. Noel and I sat quietly watching the traffic scream past.

'I think we would have had to cross here to continue,' pointed Noel.

I was horrified; it was a large road-way that crossed the highways!

It has to get better, I thought.

The showground gates were locked. We could walk into the ground but not drive. About five hundred metres from the entrance was a flat area allocated for BNT trekkers. Bit by bit, we moved our gear.

As we set up Stevie and commenced our backwards and forwards trips, a smartly dressed lady passed by walking two friendly dogs.

'Hello,' she said. 'What are you two up to?'

'We're doing the BNT and staying here for a while; one of our boys has a bruised back,' I said, as I continued to load Stevie.

'Oh dear,' said the friendly face. 'Well, I'll let you get on – you look busy.' And she strolled off with her dogs wagging their tails in tow.

With all the gear near the campsite, the boys wanted to eat, so we let them go, thinking they'd just stand there and eat. They were tired; with food at their feet, where would they go? Well, they were free; they had a new place to explore – tired? – pah – *they* weren't tired. It was just us who were perpetually knackered.

It would have been fine, had they just wandered around a bit and then found more grass to eat. But, no, it was more fun to head towards the narrow entrance that led to a road. They had no reason to go there; there was no food in that part. And they didn't like narrow entrances. Noel raced over so they couldn't get out. So as to foil him, they decided to split up and trot in different directions around the arena. This sent them silly, as they couldn't work out why they were becoming farther apart from each other. Eventually we caught the ringleader, Charlie, and nabbed Ned. Soon the others surrendered, and we tied them up while we made their paddock with the electric fence. We ferried the water, and they settled in nicely, eating, drinking, and relaxing. We set about making up our camp.

There were two scruffy huts; at one end a new shed was under construction. A roof stretched out between the old shacks; beneath it was a rather convenient concrete floor with timber benches. We gratefully stacked our equipment under the roof, utilised the benches, and pitched the tent behind it, within reasonable privacy. Soon the camp was up, and Noel lit a fire. We relaxed in the knowledge that we weren't moving for a while. Dom needed rest and so did we.

In the village near the showground there was one tiny, sparsely-stocked shop with hefty pricing. I bought the last loaf of bread, a bottle of wine, and some munchies. I indulged in a piece of chicken, which was ridiculously expensive. However, we'd been living on Snickers and, in the evening, soup or noodles. We deserved a little decadence.

We sat around the campfire, on one of the wooden benches, the green peeling paint suiting our circumstances. I hadn't been drinking enough water, and this was becoming a problem. We carried water in our saddle-bags, but the more I drank, the more I peed. I don't mind peeing behind a bush. But getting on and off Charlie was a big effort. I guided him into dips to make it a little easier. But we were doing so much road work there were few places with privacy.

After a few sips of wine, I could feel the warmth returning to my cheeks in a hectic red. Dehydration, fatigue, and relief were a heady emotional cocktail that added to the merriment. Our belts had been tightened – literally, stamina was down, and we were both under-nourished. We laughed, we cried, and we ate and drank and slipped into a wonderful deep sleep.

The next morning I woke up with a migraine, something I suffer with from time to time. This one squeezed my head. I winced when I moved. If I wasn't careful it would lead to vomiting. But I was desperate for a shower. Noel had already been up and put the kettle on (I managed to swallow some painkillers and tea). I put the little gas stove on to boil water for the shower bag. Noel smelt wonderfully clean. He'd checked the boys and topped up their water. I prepared my shower bag and knew I'd feel better once clean. There was a convenient tree behind the new shed. As I looped the string of the heavy bag onto a branch, I heard a car but thought that Noel would keep anyone away. As I peeled off layers, trucks started to enter the showground, and a few bodies turned up.

'Who are you? And what are you doing here?' I heard an unfriendly voice say. I pulled my jumper back on and sighed. No shower for me.

'We are trekking along the BNT, and...'

'Get out, this is the Pony Club's area; you have no right being here!'

'We have every right to be here – read the sign.' Noel pointed to the board that indicated this spot was for BNT campers. He was keeping marvellously calm. He may not have been cool inside. He stood still, erect, not backing down.

'We have a show on the showground today, today the showground is ours, and you *have* to leave and take your horses too!' the unpleasant man continued.

I had turned away; this man makes me mad to this day. He was lucky I had a migraine, I wouldn't have been as calm as Noel. I could hardly move my head, the pain pinched nerves, and my anger was building, but talking would be a real struggle. I'd have to leave this one up to Noel.

'That's not right. The showground people know we are here. We have every right to be here,' Noel repeated. The other man walked off in a huff.

We gathered up our gear from under the shelter where they were setting up. Admittedly, we had left our equipment in a bit of disarray; we had spread out and indulged in all the covered space.

Our tent was directly behind the shelter, and this rather unfriendly Pony Club set up their tables and chairs in front of us – ensuring their backs were firmly placed in our direction.

If they'd only known; I grew up in Pony Club, and I knew all about it, what they do and how they do it. Once my head had cleared, I would have been delighted to be a part of the day. I have run many shows such as these. I could have been a marvellous help and enjoyed the day. Instead this Pony Club would be remembered as full of ignorant and arrogant people. So much for horsey folk being kindred spirits! The judges and admin gathered in the shelter and made a point of ignoring us. Not one person said, 'G'day.'

We had moved our gear, but our boys were corralled off near the main arena. Then another guy came over. He'd obviously been sent to move us along.

'The showground is ours today; we have hired it,' he explained. 'If you move your horses into the pens they can stay.'

At this point, I am sure steam came out of my ears. Our boys had worked hard. The pens were just bare mud with no grass. Were they supposed to stand there all day and eat nothing? Fortunately, Noel translated my thoughts into words as if he had read my mind. My head was pounding.

'Okay,' the guy eventually agreed, or gave up. 'But they can't stay where they are; people will be parking there.' And with that, we watched as a stream of horse trucks snaked their way into the grounds.

We agreed to move the horses as far away as we could, and we did, in a corner with grass and where they were safe. They watched the comings and goings with interest.

By this time my headache hadn't worsened but hadn't improved either. It was still touch and go which way it'd go. The day was chilly, and we donned beanies and jackets and sat on a bench to watch the events. There was nothing else we could do.

I buried my head in my coat and indulged in misery. We sat in silence. I felt grubby.

'Hello again,' said a cheery voice. 'What are all these people doing on your camping ground?'

The lady with the dogs we had seen briefly yesterday reappeared. We explained the morning's events.

After a brief pause, she said, 'I know, why don't you come home with me? You can have a hot shower and a cuppa.'

My eyes glistened with welling tears, and a big grin spread across my face.

'Oh my goodness, that would be amazing – thank you!'

I was worried that I'd get to her house and start being ill. But there was something about Anne, something down-to-earth and realistic, like wearing a colourful scarf that matches everything; we were instantly comfortable in her company.

We checked the boys, grabbed our wallets, and jumped into Anne's car. I sat in the back and was promptly cuddled by Tyson and Bridie, who thought it great fun to have a human sit with them stroking their backs. They fought for my attention on the ten-minute drive back to Anne's neat house.

'Right, the kettle's on, here's some fresh towels, there's the shower. Make yourselves at home; I'm popping out.' She swept up her keys, spun around with her short blonde hair trying to keep up, stepped through the front door, and disappeared.

Noel and I stood there, in shabby clothes, looking at each other. Suddenly we had been transported to a lovely house, by a kind woman, and she'd gone out! The only thing to do was to shower and try not to break anything.

The water washed the pain away; as soon as I stepped under the hot jets I groaned. The warmth relaxed my bunched shoulders, easing the tension from my head: it was utter relief. As we pulled on clean clothes, Anne strode back in with armfuls of food.

'I've bought lunch.' She grinned. 'Sit down. How do you take your tea? It's only bread, and I'll make sandwiches. Ham salad okay?'

'Perfect; anything; as it comes,' Noel and I said as one, standing together not quite believing where we were.

'I can't thank you enough,' I said to Anne. 'This is so kind of you; we should be making *you* lunch!'

'Not at all. I've travelled a lot; I can understand how awful it is to be treated so appallingly, *and* when you are visitors in our town!' Her frown accompanied the tutting.

We sat with Anne for a few hours. Instant and firm friendships were formed that day. Anne became our saviour in more ways than one: she became our support, our rock. Never had a person come into our lives so suddenly, so warmly, that we love so dearly.

Anne became an honorary member of the team. She's a resourceful lady, having done much travelling herself with her family. Now, her two dogs kept her occupied, and then we came along to fill any gaps of time she may or may not have had! She was a mine of information.

'Okay, you two,' she said with pen raised, 'what do you need? How can I help you? I have phone, internet, contacts: what's first?' Anne's no-nonsense kindness was exactly what we needed.

'I've been worrying about the boys,' I explained. 'They look happy and have shiny coats, but we can't seem to cover their ribs.'

'They look grand to me,' Anne commented.

'Yes, I don't think they're suffering, but we ought to get their teeth rasped before we set off, and of course arrange the vet check, and we can get Dom's back looked at too.'

'Easily done,' said Anne, and before we knew it the vet visit was arranged.

Hall has another remarkable lady in residence. We'd heard about Jan from other folk. She's a vet who doesn't take payment! Yes, you read that right. Her passion is animals. She charges whatever the drugs cost her. She doesn't take payment for her time, or make money on medications. It probably won't surprise you to learn that many other vets have tried to put her out of business. But she battles on. Every day there's a long winding queue outside her home (and clinic) with people cradling their animals that are in need of care. Of course, she does visits, and Anne said we couldn't find a better vet for our horses.

As we had adopted the boys, the SPPHA regulations required us to arrange six-month and twelve-month vet checks (for the first year only, if they passed, then officially we owned them). We had almost reached the six-month check for Spirit; the others weren't far behind. So the SPPHA kindly agreed that they could be checked together.

Jan's not a people person. That's not to say she doesn't like people, or is rude. But you can just see and sense that she thinks so much more about animals than she does of people. She's a small woman with the years of knowledge etched on her skin, who exudes wisdom. We liked her instantly. Her manner around the horses immediately put us all at ease. We just knew we'd learn a lot from this lady.

She followed the rules of the vet check, grading the boys and giving them the once over. Many moons ago, when I had my first horses, they could smell a vet a mile away and became agitated. Our boys didn't bat an eye-lid. They weren't restless or worrisome; they were perfectly behaved. They passed the check, but Jan agreed that they did need a bit more weight on them and a teeth check would be appropriate.

'Can you please look at Dom's back too?' I asked. 'We bruised it by having his pack too tight, cinched at the top.' I cringed, hoping she didn't think that we were unworthy of being the horses' carers.

She prodded and poked, walked him up and down, and checked Dom out thoroughly. Dom loves people and enjoyed the attention. Being the youngest and newest member, he was certainly fifth in line in the pecking order. So to have all of us around him, with all the attention, he was in his element.

'Oh, yes, he's certainly bruised,' Jan said, as she stroked Dom's head.

'How long will it take to heal?' I asked, dreading the answer.

'A couple of weeks, maybe ten days.' Which was similar to what I had said when I found the bruising.

'What if we left him unloaded? Is he okay to walk for hours each day, if he carried nothing?'

'Sure,' she said, 'that'd be no problem for him; he's a lovely fella.' She smiled at Dom while stroking his ears.

Jan spent over an hour with us; she found a bit of scurf in Neddy's tail and said she'd drop in a wash later. She wouldn't take any payment, except for the wash. She had just vet-checked five big horses, administered medication, and diagnosed. All she wanted was $10 for the wash!

We forced $100 onto her. Others donated meals, shopping, and gifts in payment; we couldn't do that. The cost of this visit would have run into hundreds usually.

'This guy's not cheap, but he's good,' Jan said, as she handed us the number of a horse-dentist.

With the boys' vet-check paperwork signed, I bundled it up and mailed it to the Association. One job done, I then prepared myself for the dentist.

Horse dentists use a contraption that looks like a prop in a medieval torture movie. A 'mouth-opener' fits onto the horse's head attached with horrifying-looking brackets and catches. It keeps the horse's mouth open while the dentist sticks an enormous rasp and half his arm right up into the horse's head. Horse's teeth go a long way back. The mouth opener must, therefore, be strong.

We had no idea if our boys had ever had this done, or how they would react. Having horses' teeth rasped should be a regular

113

occurrence, but some horse owners don't bother. It's like people: some need to go to the dentist more than others.

The dentist knew how to handle horses and fidgety owners. He politely manoeuvred me out of the way and continued with the job himself. All our boys just stood there, their eyes popped a little with the rasping, as would mine. Neddy and Dom decided that walking backwards would help. I tried to calm them and keep them still. The dentist took over and gently walked with the fidgeting horses as they circled backwards in steady arcs.

He continued a soft stream of chatter, sometimes directed at the horses, sometimes at me. He kept his tone low, slow, rhythmic, and calming.

Thirty minutes later it was done, ninety Australian dollars per horse mind, but I didn't care – they were okay, and he said he'd rasped down one or two sharp teeth. These teeth can not only be painful but also prevent the horse chewing properly, stopping the animal from gaining full benefit from the scanty grass available on the trail.

Spirit – intelligent and playful

Noel on Spirit leading Stevie – Kangaroo Valley

The arrival of Dom in his winter coat – Kangaroo Valley

Neddy's not too happy with is packs – Kangaroo Valley

Charlie & Ned, Dom in background – Kangaroo Valley

Sweet – 'little' - Dommie

(l to r) Dom, Stevie, Spirit, Ned, Charlie – Kangaroo Valley

Charlie and Ned – Kangaroo Valley

Jackie riding Ned, leading Charlie

Neddy-boy – interested in what's going on - Taralga

Dom waiting to be unpacked at Crookwell Showground

Noel on Charlie – beautiful (both of them!) - Crookwell

Communications in a TSR

Trying the new packs on Stevie – Hall Showground

Jackie, Sue and Bill

The boys looking over at Canberra (l to r) Stevie, Spirit, Dom, Charlie & Ned

Inside the corrugated hut – they are all the same – basic but luxurious!

Spirit and Dom nuzzle Noel while he sleeps – Mount Clear

Oldfields Hut

Ned happier with the new packs – near Yaouk

Hiding feed in a copse of trees at Denison

Time out for a drink – Noel and his team (Spirit nearest)

Noel and his team crossing a creek – Dom on the left is about to roll!

Noel map reading (Dom nearest)
Australia's high plains

En route to Providence after leaving Horse Gully hut
Jackie on Charlie crossing the creek

16

Police Assistance

Once the boys were all checked, we left them to munch their way around the showground. We ordered hay and good quality feed, and all was well – that is until Dom choked.

It had happened before, but this time I didn't have a hose at hand. Noel had walked down to the cold showers, I had dished out the evening feed for the boys, and while they gratefully gorged, I spread their hay around. We pulled the compact sections of hay into small, thinned-out piles, to try to prevent them from gulping it.

Then suddenly Dom was on the ground, distress pulling at his eyes: he'd not gone down before. I ran my hands over his throat and found a large ball of hay that was stuck.

'You bloody idiot!' I muttered as calmly as I could through gritted teeth; I didn't need to make him any tenser. I ran back to the camp, grabbed a cup, and filled it with water, grateful that there was a tap nearby.

Sprinting back to Dom, I tried to soothe him as he became agitated.

'Steady, boy, you're okay, steady.' Lifting the cup to his lips, I used my other hand to raise his head as high as I could. I poured the water down his throat – well, some of it. I did this twice more, and suddenly he stood up, shook himself off, and started to eat again.

My adrenaline eased as I spread out the hay even further, trying to slow down their eating. As Noel returned, I slumped on the floor like a puddle and let him kick the hay around a bit more.

'We need to arrange an emergency call between us,' I said. We usually called a loud 'cooooooeeeeee' to each other when seeking the other out (works great in supermarkets) – the 'eeeeeee' goes up high and carries well.

'How about three long, loud, quick 'cooooooeeeeeees?''

'Good idea: that signal means drop everything immediately and come right now, emergency.'

'Sounds good to me.'

We both stood in silence watching the boys eat, thinking about real and imagined horrors that may cause us to make this call. We'd almost shot Spirit in an emergency – would we have another?

The days were so full. The builder working on the new shed on the showground was interested in our boys. We received many visitors, and the kettle perpetually bubbled while cups were assembled. The BNT coordinator paid us a visit.

'I've bought some ointment for your boy,' he said, looking around our camp. 'You said he has a sore back.'

I grinned, not knowing what to say; then the penny dropped.

'Oh, I've confused you, I am sorry,' I said, rather sheepishly. 'I refer to our horses as our boys!'

'Oh,' he laughed, 'I thought you had a son with you!'

'Goodness, no! These boys here are my family.'

Anne was a regular visitor, and we were spoiled rotten when she turned up. Her happy dogs, cheery smile, and delicious homemade cakes always brightened our days. She even brought us a few fabulous, homemade dinners. Where had this angel come from? To top it all, our friendship had reached a pivotal point. Anne tells it how it is, a refreshing attitude and easy to be with. So we weren't worried about asking her for some more help. If she didn't want to, she'd say.

'We're thinking about changing our packs,' Noel explained to Anne. 'And we need to find a camping shop: are you up for being our tour guide? We'll pay your petrol, shout you lunch...?'

'Absolutely, when would you like to go? No petrol money or food needed; it'll be great fun. Now, let me get my map out – I know just the place.'

We'd off-loaded ten kilos of equipment at Crookwell but then taken on almost that weight in boots for the boys. When there was a rare grass track, they could go barefoot, but we still had to carry the boots. The hard plastic panniers were driving us nuts. They were great to sit on and use as tables when in camp but too big and bulky to lift on without a struggle. We needed to lighten the load further and create a slicker system. We'd sat and thought about what we could do.

'What about backpacks?' I said, thinking out loud. 'We could have four on each horse, two each side.'

I could see Noel's brain churning over this idea. 'They have straps to hook them on,' he said thoughtfully.

'Yes, and we could lift them ourselves, as in one person could lift them. Arranging the gear into compartments – galley gear, sleeping gear, etc. – might make life easier. Actually, all the sleeping gear could go on top,' I said. The idea was gaining momentum, and we had light waterproof bags for the sleeping gear. Both Noel and I found that living out of bags was harder than we'd imagined. It wasn't like a vast, gaping cupboard with a large swinging door. Every item we needed meant minutes of frustrating rummaging. Bags could be emptied, but you then had to put everything back to keep it dry and safe from critters. When you are aching from riding all day, famished, and worn out, this becomes tedious.

We calculated that exchanging the plastic panniers for lighter bags would save us ten kilos! We had forgotten how heavy they were when empty. The tent had to go too. Instead of a two-

131

man tent (well, actually a questionable three-man), plus the canopy, we decided on two light-weight single tents. We already had a square of canvas to cover the gear. That was another few kilos saved. We were on a roll.

'We'll be looking for something for Charlie, too,' said Noel, glancing at me pointedly.

'What do you mean?' I asked innocently, knowing full well what he meant.

'You need to be able to control him better: you've fallen off once, and he is using his big head to his advantage.' Noel was right.

'Okay'

With light-bulbs flashing above our heads, we set off with Anne to seek out new equipment. A new spring lifted our steps; this would improve the system immensely.

At the first shop, we found just what we wanted. But it took hours to decide on brands, size, and set up. We found two small tents that combined saved us six kilos in comparison to our large tent. We discovered colourful backpacks, waterproof and tough, slightly smaller than we wanted, but not by much. We purchased eight in total, four for Dom, four for Spirit. That meant we could get shot of the plastic panniers completely. We still had the two canvas panniers, which were fine for Ned or Dom.

The expense wasn't a worry – it had to be done. Our thoughts were focused on making sure the boys were comfortable and free from injury. Then the journey would improve for us all.

With renewed vigour, we treated ourselves to a milkshake and cake and romped home to discard as much gear as we could. It was great teamwork between the three of us.

We stream-lined our gear; we were beyond bare-minimum. Placing a few light items in our new bags, we tried out the new system on Stevie and Spirit.

These two boys were wonderful to experiment on, so calm and trusting. We lifted up the saddles and hooked on the new bags. We had purchased climbers' clips and found that it all snapped on with little adjustment. It was so easy. We led them around. I swear Spirit lifted his head and smiled and said, *It's about time you two figured it out*. No longer did he have an enormous load up high, but a neat, tight pack. It was brilliant!

We whittled down more gear and were so stream-lined we could leave Dom free from carrying anything for a while. Ned would carry the boots, horse feed, tarp cover, and a few other lighter items, which all sat within buckets that slotted into the canvas bags. Spirit took the rest (Anne would be helping us with her car for the next couple of stops). They all carried less than forty kilos each. Ned hauled around twenty kilos depending whether their boots were on their hooves or in the bags and how much food we had.

Hall was a useful stop for so many reasons, including having the opportunity to train the boys (and us) to cope with cavallettis. These are six or eight large wooden poles lying anywhere between four and twenty inches off the ground, spaced about half a metre apart, or thereabouts. They are solid and in place to prevent cars entering the trail – presumably cyclists and horse riders could. At Hall they had a set of these poles by the entrance gate. We utilised an afternoon to introduce them to the boys. Stevie, Spirit, Dom, and Ned didn't worry about them at all. Charlie sort of skipped over a few. They worried him a little, and he figured that if he dashed over them, he'd be okay. However, he tripped and banged his legs, so I had to calm him down and teach him that it was safer and easier to take them slowly. He gradually listened, but with a little distraction, he'd trip and panic and race over them, which made him trip more.

When facing cavallettis on the trail, we now knew they could traverse them without much of a problem... or so we thought!

Charlie had 'pulled away' from me a few times. He didn't take off, but rather, if I'd asked him to stand and he spotted a rather juicy piece of grass somewhere, or wanted to start moving, with his myopic self-interest he'd push his enormous nose out, extend his neck, and pull the reins through my hands. By the time his neck was fully extended, I didn't have the strength or leverage to pull him back. I absolutely doted on this boy and found it amusing, but Noel could see potential danger.

'He'll put you in peril soon by doing that.'

And Noel's words made me come up short. I knew deep-down, that it could become hazardous. I had to find something to help me gain back control when I needed it.

We looked at bit-less bridles, contraptions that squeeze the nostrils and provide better leverage. This equipment has to be used carefully, with a gentle hand. I'd used them before on one of my horses years ago, a horse that had a mouth like a brick.

But we were trying to go bare-foot and bit-less without having anything too harsh (all the boys wore rope halters). And the largest size in the shop didn't come close to fitting Charlie's enormous head. The shop assistant didn't believe us when we told her the draught horse size wasn't big enough!

At the back of the shop we found a 'Dually Halter,' which has an additional soft rope looped over the nose. That nose-piece extended through the head-collar's side buckles, specifically so the reins could attach to it. It would provide the necessary leverage on Charlie's nose. And they had his size – 'suitcase size,' we laughed. It was a smart blue head-collar with control, all for ninety Australian dollars, thank you much. It wasn't about looking good though – it was about safety.

Another event was due to arrive at the showground, so we moved the boys to a back paddock. They weren't in sight, which I didn't like, but they had food and water.

A few days later we met Diana, another local woman from Hall. Daily she walked her dogs in the showground and invited us to dinner; we must have looked underfed. That evening we ate the most delicious roast lamb feast that was nothing short of sublime. Every mouthful melted with ease; it was just what we needed. Compared to the Pony Club, the locals were treating us beautifully.

We spent as much time as we could with Anne; we loved it when she popped in for tea (always armed with cake), until finally we had no more excuses to stay.

We checked the route on foot and found that from the showground we took a short trek alongside a highway and then crossed a huge, busy intersection of sixteen lanes, criss-crossing the lights. The trucks thundered along. We watched and tried to come up with a plan. We could cross two roads and wait on the verge between four lanes of fast traffic. I could see the boys panicking and didn't like it at all. So I rang the police.

'We have five horses and two riders, and we are loaded with gear – is there any way you could assist, just at the intersection?'

'We'll do our best: it all depends what's happening on the day, but we'll make a note. Call us on the morning you need us, about ten minutes before you want to cross.'

And so we did.

Anne came along for the ride. She parked nearby and stood with us on the bank and waited. I rang the police again.

'No problem, we'll be there in five minutes.'

I grinned; what a relief.

As promised, two police turned up, a male and female. They looked at us, looked at the road, and looked back at us. A small discussion ensued between them and then a phone-call. They'd waved at us, but didn't say a word.

Within two minutes every single traffic light turned red, the police turned to us, smiled, and beckoned us over. Anne came along for the fun.

'Take my camera, Anne; I can't miss this opportunity!' She ran alongside, in front and behind, snapping away.

Noel and I felt like royalty. The horses seemed to give a horse-shrug and obeyed our command to set off diagonally across the centre of lights.

'Thanks so much, that's just brilliant!' I yelled out to the police.

'Cheers, cobber,' called Noel.

We wore huge grins and waved at all the cars and thanked them, while urging our boys on. From here on out, there was a grass passage right off the road - a blessed relief.

On the opposite corner, we stopped on a large, safe verge. We collected our camera from Anne and waved farewell to the police and Anne as the traffic commenced its rush.

It was time for our first 'live' test of walking over the cavallettis. With only the slightest hesitation, each boy walked perfectly over the obstacles. They were low, though, lower than those at Hall, but we were glad to have had the practice: now we were safe, on grass, and clear of traffic.

'This is great, what a buzz!'

'Yeah, I couldn't believe the coppers did that for us, what a service.'

The boys had their heads up with fervour, keenness. They were thriving on this journey, their coats were gleaming, and they had bonded with each other as well as us, accepting their roles within the troop. I still felt the need to cover their ribs with a little more fat: I like to feel the ribs, but not see them. They weren't poking out though. But the shine on their pelts and in their eyes meant they were doing okay. I had to learn to chill out a bit more.

'Great idea practicing on those cavallettis at the showground,' I said to Noel. 'That saved us a lot of bother.'

'Yeah, I can see them trusting us and believing that we are doing the right thing for them when we ask them to do something for us. It's incredible to be a part of that,' he said wistfully. 'I'm starting to understand that bond you tried to explain before, with the horses.'

This was a shorter day, as we had arranged to stay with Belconnen Pony Club. The next 'official' camp was around thirty kilometres away, and that was too far for us. Via Anne's generosity, we'd driven to the Pony Club, and asked them if they could help. They were delighted to assist. We trekked across reserves, avoiding roads for twenty kilometres to Belconnen.

We met the club manager on arrival, who opened up the shed, made us welcome, and left us to get on with it, offering us use of the tea and coffee too. We had a kettle, comfy couches, and shelter. The boys were safe and had all they needed, a real blessing for us! The only stipulation was to clear the paddock of poo piles before we left.

As we were so close to Anne's home, she had carried some of our gear and met us there in the evening. We shared a cup of tea and didn't want her to leave.

'I'll take some gear to the next stop too,' she offered.

'That'd be wonderful!'

We left the next day. Anne was with us during the morning, helping us pack and marvelling at all the gear and time it took.

'See you in Yarralumla,' she said with a wave.

We walked for a few hours, the new packs didn't move, and the horses were happy. We received so many compliments on how well the boys behaved and how fit and healthy they looked. Dom thought he was on holiday, and we had a good day, until...

We turned left into a small side road. There was a large metal gate and a set of cavallettis to traverse. Noel's boys had been walking in a straight line, one after the other, all the way. Noel lined them up, and Stevie stepped over the poles. Spirit duly followed, and at the last minute a butterfly, or some-such silly thing, caught Dom's eye, and he wandered off to the left. He meandered too far, and as Spirit was jigging over the poles, in his swing, half a tonne of muscle momentum, he pulled Dom's lead rope, Dom's head jerked forward, and he leaped to catch up and collided with the gate! The gate rattled. Spirit pulled forward and shoved his ears back; the lead rope on his gear was pulling him back. Meanwhile, Dom's head was being yanked forward, over the gate.

'Grab, Spirit,' I yelled. 'Get him to stop.'

Noel jumped off Stevie and tried to calm Spirit. He was half-way through the poles and was not happy that he had to stop right there.

I'm gonna break my legs if this keeps up, you could almost hear him say.

Meanwhile Dom tried to pull Spirit backwards.

Spirit became agitated and angry and pulled forward while trying to step over the poles.

Dom was panicking and pulling back.

The steel gate was bending under Dom's weight, and Dom's legs were about to climb up the rungs.

Our quick release catches hadn't sprung!

I was about to jump off Charlie when Noel leaped at Dom with a knife and sliced through the rope. The lead rope parted, and the metal tag smashed into Noel's hand.

Dom relaxed and looked around as if to say, *What the heck happened there?*

Spirit shook himself and straightened up as if it was all rather undignified.

None of them were hurt. Spirit had a small graze on a hind leg, where the last pole had caught him when Dom started to pull back. Dom was eating now as if nothing had happened. Noel's hand was already blue. My heart eased down to a mild gallop.

All this happened in about twenty seconds, but it felt like two hours. Noel tied up Stevie and Spirit and led Dom over without any problems.

Meanwhile, Charlie had become bored and was eager to join his buddies. He hated being apart, and he danced from foot to foot. I made sure Ned's head was next to my knee and he had enough space to step through without his bags snagging, and we walked across. Charlie upped the pace, and it was hard to settle him back. But there were no problems.

'Right, we'd better not take them over three at a time,' Noel said.

'Yes,' I agreed, the self-reproach still nagging with my inept decisions and lack of fore-thought. Three horses leading in a line is quite something; they had been doing it so well, I took it for granted. I had also forgotten that Dom was just a baby and would easily be distracted. We were lucky to have the boys in one piece without injury. What was I thinking?

We had two or three more of the cavallettis that day. Each time, I held Dom while Noel took Stevie and Spirit across. Then he tied them up and took Dom over by himself. I then took Ned and Charlie over. It was time we didn't have. It would take ten to fifteen minutes to dismount, get organised, tie them up safely, reconnect, mount up, and get going. The flow of the ride was broken, and it slowed us down.

Noel wanted to chainsaw all cavallettis!

17

Personality Changes

I was looking forward to staying in Yarralumla. Our guidebook described the campsite as being 'right next to the zoo.' I'd also read other trekkers had 'watched the tigers' from their campsite.

Either the campsite had moved or the zoo had.

As we skirted around Canberra, we climbed up ridges and trekked past suburban backyards. As if by rote, the sunny day motivated lawn-mowing, and a particularly large sit-on machine gave pause for thought to one of our boys. Stevie went with the ebb and flow of each day; he'd tackled the daily challenges presented to him without hesitation, until we met lawn mowers. It was interesting that the other boys ignored them. But as the square buzzing machine headed towards Stevie, he stopped dead.

'It's okay, Stevie,' Noel said, his voice betraying an awkward combination of conviction and fear. If Stevie freaked out, he had two other boys tied to him, to drag along. Noel didn't need another knitting session.

Stevie appeared to swallow his growing anxiety and followed Charlie and Ned, who didn't worry one bit! Noel's troop veered away from the machine, giving the buzzing metal as wide a berth as they possibly could, Stevie leading the way with his two companions left with no choice but to follow.

Being so close to Canberra meant busy roads. Fortunately, there are still great tracks to follow, mostly shared with cyclists. We were glad we were trekking on the trail now, before Canberra sucked up every piece of vegetation.

A new challenge awaited; we had to convince the boys to walk beneath highways. We reached our first tunnel. The cars above vibrated an echo throughout the concrete passageway. The boys stopped as if to say, *You're kidding, right?*

The tunnels were low, so we dismounted. Having us walk in first, leading the boys, gave them the confidence they needed. It was the trust we had all developed in each other. You could almost feel the boys shrug and say, *Well, if that's what they reckon...* Cautiously, and with wide-eyes, they followed us in, the hooves striking the concrete floor and creating several dozen clip-clopping echoes, while the bridge shook above our heads.

With the horses' ears flicking to and fro, we all walked through together and suddenly popped out the other side, breaking back into bright sunlight. The boys perked up their heads, and their eyes twinkled with achievement.

The trek took us through the Arboretum, which should have been pleasant and peaceful; instead it was hot, frustrating, and lengthy. The maps weren't clear, or at least we couldn't understand them. Finally, we received instructions from an employee working on the grounds. We still rode for several more kilometres than necessary. The pathway leading out of the tree plantation was hidden and could be found by many different routes – we found the longest.

We sedately trekked alongside the Molonglo River and crossed over to climb a short hill to the TSR. I marvelled at little Neddy. At times when Charlie hesitated at a bridge or dark path, Ned would take the first steps. Even though he was led, it was as if he rolled his eyes at Charlie and said, *What now?*

In the afternoon, Noel was searching for his sleeveless jacket.

'I haven't seen it,' I said. 'Weren't you wearing it this morning?'

'Yes, I was.' Noel frowned, his hand atop his head, as if it would help him think. 'With all that mounting and dismounting, I think I laid it over a pack and it's fallen off – I've lost it.'

This was irritating: every last item was important to us, whatever it was. There were no superfluous articles. Another entry was added to the shopping list.

Although we had a safe paddock – two in fact – there was no grass, and my heart fell. But the boys had water, freedom, and safety. We could view the city from here and stay as long as we liked. The TSR had a drop toilet too, which was great, as there was little other privacy. We were on top of a hill in company with just a bit of scrubby bush.

We opened the rusty gate and led the horses to the trough and tap. While they were having their fill, Spirit showed his impatience with carrying his pack by rolling on the ground. He was down before we noticed! Fortunately, he only broke some biscuits and dented the small petrol canister. We were planning to change this container as I wasn't happy with carrying petrol for the stove – I could smell it, and it worried me. We unpacked, made camp, and called Anne. We were still near Anne's house, and we had agreed to meet here.

'Is there anything you need, anything at all?' she asked.

'Well, I hate to ask,' I said feeling a bit cheeky, 'but would you mind putting a bale of hay in the back of your car? There's not much grass here.' I cringed as I thought I was pushing my luck.

'Not at all, why only one?' she said. 'That won't last long. I'll tell you what, I'll hook up the trailer. How many bales shall I bring?'

This woman was a marvel, and a few hours later, there she was with hay, feed, cake, dinners, and a wee nip of something to say 'cheers' together with. Not only that, she had found us with our rather dubious instructions! We sat together, relaxed and happy, listening to the roar of lions from the hidden zoo that was carried along by the breeze.

It was here that advice we received in the early days came back to me: 'Watch out for wild pigs; they'll bail you up.'

We'd seen three wild horses so far, kangaroos, one snake (that crossed the road in front of us), a bull, and not much else in wildlife terms. My mind wandered to other advice too: 'Don't wash up in cold water; it will make you ill.' This made me smile; we were one step away from wiping our plastic cutlery under our arm-pits and counting that as washing up! But, of course, we didn't. However, we did wash up in cold soapy water. We had done so for nine years on our first sailing boat, so we knew it would be fine.

Soon the boys became restless after clearing the paddocks of anything edible, and they came back to the camp to ask for more food. I had to ration the hay supply; together they could munch through a square bale in minutes. Across the narrow laneway there was a wonderful cross-country course that was open to everyone. I marvelled at the array of rustic jumps on offer. I found it incredible that the local authority maintained this land for the public – for such a dangerous (but fun) sport. It was brilliant. The jumps had been constructed in a paddock brimming with lush grass. So we made up a corral to one side. Our boys were out of the way and able to eat great food. I didn't like not having them in my view from our camp, but they were happy enough. Food was far more important than my comfort levels.

We left Yarralumla after a few days and headed down the other side of the hill into a large horse yard. We stopped and asked directions, but no one could decipher our maps either.

'Head on out past the arenas, I am pretty sure it's that way.' Each person we asked pointed in a different direction.

We steered the horses towards an arena and continued out to the road. We stood beside the highway for ten minutes trying to work out where to go. Finally, we crossed and found a track, and it was here it all turned horrid.

We'd spent two hours trekking two kilometres. The next camp was a good twenty-five kilometres away. We couldn't waste any time. We were tense, lost, and hot, and this snowballed into a frightful row.

I called the park ranger and explained our predicament.

'According to our maps, we are a couple of kilometres from a park: can we stop there for the night?' I asked hopefully.

'No, sorry,' he said. 'Even if I allowed it, I'd receive no end of complaints from the residents nearby.'

This fuelled the worry, and when Spirit's pack slipped, Noel became irritated. I retaliated with anger. Usually, if one of us is irate or mean, the other isn't, and arguments are avoided. We balance each other out. This time, we had both hit rock-bottom and clashed ferociously.

What proceeded was a massive argument, resulting in true feelings being revealed.

'I'm not enjoying this,' yelled Noel. 'It's not what I expected; it's not fun!'

'Well, I don't want to stop,' I hollered back.

'We had an agreement: if one of us wanted to stop the trip, the other had to stop too!'

'Well, I don't want to, I can't,' I shouted.

For ten minutes, we argued back and forth while Noel struggled to re-arrange Spirit's pack.

By now, we'd eaten into almost three hours of trekking time; we wouldn't make the next camp, even if the packs stayed where they should and we didn't lose our way.

'I'm turning back!' Noel said angrily. I had to agree: we had no choice. So with our tails between our legs and minds fuming, we trekked back to Yarralumla. We had travelled just four kilometres!

The trek allowed us both to cool down, but I didn't want to stop. When Noel makes up his mind, it is usually a done thing. I desperately wanted to carry on, to figure this out. The thought of stopping and working out what to do with the boys broke my heart.

I wasn't ready to go to England; a new trainer had taken over at work, and I didn't want to return to teaching just yet. I didn't want to fail either. I couldn't really care what other people thought, but I knew *I'd* regret giving up. *Would I have the time to return another day?* I pondered, but that thought squeezed my heart. *I want to do it with my boys now!*

I didn't really fret about age eventually becoming a barrier, even though every single muscle was squealing quite regularly. I am aware of my body aging but, generally I feel fit and healthy, and I have plans to stay this way well into several more decades. Believing in staying healthy is the first step, I think, to actually staying that way.

Back at the paddock, I looked at the boys. They looked wonderful, as if they had been polished. I had to carry on for them and for me. I hadn't conquered this yet. And sadly, my emotions were so overwhelming, I thoughtlessly disregarded Noel's feelings.

'I don't want to carry on,' Noel explained. 'I'm just not enjoying it.'

'Well, I do!'

'We had an agreement...'

'I don't care, I can't stop, I won't stop, the boys don't want to stop,' I said beneath the tears that were plopping down my face. 'I will manage all five: you can go home.'

'We don't have a home – what am I supposed to do?'

'I don't know. I want to carry on; you can meet me in the car,' I said, my mind working overtime to try to figure this out.

'I don't want to do that.'

This silliness became epic and continued as we set up the tents and made the beds. I then hid in my tent. The tears continued: tears for the wretched, frequent arguing; tears with the thought of *what now*; and self-pitying tears.

'Do you want some of this?' Noel asked calmly. A few hours had passed, and Noel had made some dinner – a peace offering perhaps?

'Okay.' We sat in silence for a while. I swallowed some pain-killers, an event that was becoming far too regular.

'You can't manage the five of them on your own,' Noel suggested lightly.

'I will; I can. I'm not stopping.'

Our energy had dried up; we had arrived at a stale-mate.

'Okay, we'll give it another go.'

Instead of feeling gratitude, despair crowded my thoughts. I had got what I wanted, but I felt shame, as though I were greedy.

'Let's give it a go, and if it doesn't work, we'll re-evaluate it again,' I said. This was my compromise, even though Noel had held out the longer olive-branch.

My fears of stopping were a jumble of hectic emotions all fighting for dominance. We had agreed that once we'd done the trail we'd go to England. We didn't know for how long, but it had to be enough time for me to be close and reconnect to my immediate family. My dad had been riding the unexpected health events of living through his seventies. I always feel he will be around forever, that everyone I know will. When I had dithered about when and for how long we'd go, Noel had said, 'the only way I can help you is to say that if you don't go when you can you may regret it; you can't see them when they've gone.' Noel lost his dad when he was twenty-five. I can almost accept I won't be alive forever, but I find it tougher to acknowledge that fact for the people I care for. I've already told Noel that I have to go before he does!

My dad, unbeknown to him, rode along with us on many days – in my head. I'd not seen him much when I was very young; he'd worked long hours. But I vividly recalled the chocolate treats he'd bring home every Friday night, and a bright yellow kitchen set he'd bought me when I'd been poorly. It made me smile to myself.

It may sound ridiculous, but I now thought of my parents as people and friends as well as Mum and Dad. That's by no means disrespectful but more towards acknowledging respect. Thinking this way reminded me they were people with feelings, emotions, fears, desires – not "just" Mum and Dad. I'd find myself thinking of them as Val and Roy, assessing their lives, what they'd endured, and mostly what they'd given me. I'd often find myself grinning while my hip joints rotated with Charlie's gait. I'd feel tears too, produced from deep gratitude, admiration, and love.

If we gave up this adventure now, what would we do? Sit the boys in a paddock so I could worry about my family full-time? It would only take one more health episode in the UK for me to go; while I was AWOL I could ignore the heart-pulls, the responsibilities. I had no pressure from home, just my own will, and it wouldn't be long until that will was torn.

We stopped for the next day while we tried to figure out which direction to go. We asked other riders and people at the yard and finally were told that the arenas we were looking at were the wrong ones.

'There are more?' I asked.

'Yes, instead of heading down to the small ones near the yard, head around them and find the other, larger arenas.'

Now we could see where we had gone wrong, and the route was clear. So the following day, we re-packed and headed off once again.

A short way down the trail, we met two horse riders coming the other way.

'Oh, brilliant,' they said, when they saw we were packing. 'How far have you come?'

'From Taralga,' I replied, proud of our achievements.

'Oh,' said the guy, with a big frown and temerity, 'well, you haven't come far, have you?'

If only he knew.

'Could you look at our map and tell us if we're in the right place please?' Noel asked, wanting to double-check, after yesterday's debacle. The riders 'ummed' and 'ahhed' and pointed in the opposite direction to where we were heading.

'Oh, you are heading towards Tharwa,' the guy continued; then he spun around one hundred eighty degrees and pointed in the opposite direction again and said, 'Head for those hills.'

Noel and I squinted in the distance: in what seemed like several hundred kilometres away, there was a bump. 'Head for there' were his directions! I looked at the man with contempt that was so thick, he must have felt it; my thoughts were singularly focused on ignoring his advice. I'm not very forgiving when I'm tired. Noel thanked the riders, and we carried on with our own ideas of navigation.

Under bridges, across roads, we made our way south. We traversed one paddock with other horses, the owners watching us with a keen eye.

'That is marvellous how they do that,' one lady said, pointing at Noel's string of three. 'Do you recommend the trail?'

Noel looked at me, his eyebrows raised in anticipation of my answer. 'Well,' I began, 'it's a lot harder than we thought, but the boys are amazing.'

'They look amazing and are so well behaved.'

We continued on, and although there were many roads to travel, the verges were wide and safe.

I carried a knot of knowledge in my stomach that we'd survive this trip together, we'd all be safe. I had to stay positive and optimistic; 'today' is the 'good old days' of tomorrow. I also had too much to do in my life, so I couldn't afford time-wasting injuries. I could see us all growing old together, and these thoughts helped me push through the tougher times.

Our next camp was at the back of a large shopping centre, so our notes told us. But first we started to experience more of Canberra's narrow gates. Some idiot behind a desk had locked all the gates so cars could not enter. Fair enough. For people using the trail by foot, horse, or bike, an official had designed a small gate, just wide enough for people, bikes, and horses that *didn't carry anything!* Our packed boys were twice as wide as normal. They just couldn't fit. Brilliant! Office bureaucracy at its best. Whoever designed these blasted gates had obviously not been on the rural route, or given the remotest thought to people using the track needing to carry gear.

It was infuriating. Unloading and loading bags was an enormous job. Not just the physical work, but the care and attention needed to ensure our boys didn't suffer rubbed or sore backs. With just the two of us, it was a real juggling act.

The boys would become restless; we'd become tired. They hated being apart, so they'd fidget (didn't you Charlie?). They didn't enjoy the bags going on and off. It upset the whole rhythm of the day, made us all cranky, and took an inordinate amount of time at each gate.

Neddy dreaded these gates: with his canvas bags he could sometimes just squeeze through – if he was dead centre, and if there weren't wire or metal protrusions sticking out.

He panicked if the bags touched the sides of the gate and ran through at full speed. His little eyes protruded wildly, and he'd run over me. Fortunately, Ned had a short memory, and as soon as he was through the gap, he relaxed and forgot all about it.

The camp site we were looking for was way back behind any shops. Our dreams of a shopping centre and perhaps a burger vanished. There were buildings in the distance. We weren't sure if we were in the right place, but after six hours of riding with the camp still to be made, we made the decision to stop.

We were sharing the muddy course with cyclists. They'd race up behind us, deathly quiet, and all of a sudden appear in a flash, both horses and riders jumping out of their skins. Why people thought it was a good idea to sneak up on five, half-tonne beasts with two little riders hanging on was beyond comprehension. Any noise – a cough, a bell, a 'hello, coming past' – would have been greatly appreciated.

We still weren't sure we were in the right place when we stopped, but time was marching on, and there was still a lot of work to do. We located a good patch of grass amongst a collection of trees to the side of the pathway. A deep creek snaked along nearby. The boys couldn't reach down into the water, but we could with the buckets, and we didn't have to carry them too far.

We spent a good hour making up the paddock with the electric fence. Thin roots swelled into trees, both obstacles to step over and around: the banks were steep.

Eventually the boys were free to roam; they sucked up a long drink and ate while watching us make our camp. They knew feed would be coming soon.

We hung the shower bag in a tree, soon refreshed by the tingling creek water; pitched the tents; stacked the gear under cover; and brewed a cup of tea. While we sipped our drinks, we boiled a packet of noodles. It sounds so easy when I write it. The boys were tolerant, but they were hungry and tired too. Our gear would usually end up spread over twenty square metres or so; then our tent site would be a bit further away. All our equipment had to be stacked up properly so it wasn't damaged and to ensure it was completely covered by the tarps: we couldn't load the boys up with wet gear. It may have been fine, but I wasn't prepared to risk it, and I wouldn't have liked a wet pad on my back with gear stacked on it.

Dom's back was now completely healed, so we planned to pack him the next day.

Noel and I gratefully crawled into bed. For once I didn't fall instantly asleep, I wrestled with my emotions. The trekking was harder than we expected, but Noel and I like challenges; I certainly feel satisfaction from pushing myself to the point of torture. This time had I gone too far? I knew Noel wasn't enjoying it and we were arguing more than we ever had. It wasn't just about being viewed as 'giving up'. There was so much more going on. I lay on my kaleidoscope of bruises and aches, and tried to reach down to my inner sentiments and manipulate my emotions into a language I could recognise.

I realised that as I had reached middle age I had become softer. I can't stand any form of cruelty, never have, but now when confronted with it I can feel my insides churn: instantly my eyes water, my heart hurts, and I become angry, incredibly angry – so much so I want to hurt the people that do the hurting. Absurdly, this also made me stronger; I'd become tougher. Intense emotions that made me weak also made me stalwart. I would not be beaten by bruises, tiredness, struggles, and monotony. Despite my injuries I had to persevere. It was far tougher than I had envisaged, but that made me want to do it more. I encounter a perverse enjoyment in doing something I'm not enjoying as much as I should be! I hate giving up on someone else's terms or for reasons beyond my control. If the journey is rough, it is also more worthwhile; the fear and anguish make the courage and contentment that much sweeter.

The swirling emotions spun in a tornado and scooted out of my belly and head and allowed me to sleep. Once again the night was gone, a void: it didn't exist. It was as though I closed my heavy eyes, turned over, wincing, and woke up to morning. I'm not great at getting up in the morning, but once awake and the realisation of where I was dawned on me, I became instantly alert; our circumstances and responsibility were like a neat shot of adrenaline. I couldn't see the boys; I couldn't hear them. I just had to check they were okay.

Fighting cramp, lack of space, and the need to pee, I stumbled and fumbled and eventually unzipped my tent to fall out the side. If I hadn't woken up during the night for a 'wee by Braille,' the urgency was somewhat heightened in the morning.

'Did you hear those people this morning?' I heard a voice come from the grey material opposite me.

'No, I didn't hear a thing.' I was grappling with my boots; trying to bend one's leg to put a boot on, while fighting cramp with a reflexive straightening of the leg, creates quite a challenge.

'Just before dawn, a torch light shone on the tents, and I heard people talking; they didn't stay long.'

That's odd, I thought. I was becoming a bit twitchy with not seeing the horses yet. I stood and looked around.

'Hi, Charlie,' I crooned. He ignored me.

'Morning, Neddy-boy.' I grinned, my eyes softening. Neddy always said hello back, even if it was just a look.

'Hello, Spirit,' I called, being completely ignored.

'Dommiiieeee! You okay, little Dommie?' I asked.

Then my stomach dropped; no Stevie.

'Stevie, Steeevvviiie! Where are you?' I hadn't quite panicked, as there were a few more trees to look around, but I was quickly marching toward the alarm threshold.

'I can't see Stevie – he's not here!' I raced up and down the bank, looked behind trees, in shadows, and then a movement caught my eye. About thirty metres outside the electric fence, Stevie raised his head and looked at me. I am sure he grinned, lowered his head, and then carried on eating.

'What are you doing out there?' I asked, but he didn't have the courtesy to reply.

The electric fence was on, it was still up, and it was too high to simply step over. He must have jumped it – or had our early morning visitors tried to take him? Was the grass better out there? It certainly didn't look like it. Stevie wasn't spooked or restless; he was perfectly happy, as were the other boys.

'Your horse is being pesky again,' I said to Noel, wearing a cheeky grin.

With his head up watching me approach, Stevie stood while I strapped on his head collar and led him back within the tribe's camp. He continued eating as if giving me complete heart-failure and several grey hairs was just an everyday occurrence – then I realised, *he's right!*

Kangaroo Training

After swallowing thick, steamy porridge and a dark cup of tea, we commenced the laborious task of packing up. It was tricky, as there was little flat ground.

Eventually, we eased into our saddles with weary sighs and set off again. As we settled into our routine, we all warmed up under the soft blues, surrounded by pretty greens: the day felt mellow, pleasant. But, before we could enjoy this too much, we had to dismount and unpack to traverse a narrow gate.

I tell you, the language from Noel and me made the boys' ears twitch. It was so frustrating. Neddy did his dash through the gate, and one of the bags caught on a piece of wire thoughtfully left to make it more of a challenge. Fortunately, it was just a small tear. We unpacked the others and led them through.

Today's event, although we didn't know it yet, would be kangaroo training. We hadn't seen many at all. I wanted to see lots; I wanted the boys to become accustomed to them – and they did, pretty much all in one day.

We were starting to circle around the back of Canberra amongst large kangaroo gatherings. Enjoying the undulations and easy life of soft ground and no cars, we skirted around a cluster of sport fields. I could see roos everywhere, not near us, but I knew we would meet some soon. I was ready. About two-hundred metres up in front were twenty roos. Charlie spotted them and hesitated; we had fenced paddocks on each side.

'Walk-on,' I said firmly, looking ahead to where I wanted to go. He did. As we were about thirty metres away, our troop halted. The kangaroos looked at us; we looked at them. They were huddled in the paddock to our right. Abruptly, one took off, and the rest followed. Our boys watched, wide-eyed, as the roos effortlessly bounded over the five-foot fence and across our path, disappearing into the bush.

'Aren't they graceful?' said Noel as he watched them hop high.

'Yes, they've amazing strength in those legs: they jump so high with such little effort!'

It was entertaining. But just as we'd uttered these few words, a kangaroo messed up his timing and perfected a clown performance. With a nonchalant bound, he was almost over. But one of his hind legs relaxed, and it hung down, snagging on the top wire of the fence. The forward momentum carried him over while he legs caught on the top. His narrow body twanged back towards the fence. Our boys lifted their heads up high, ears pricked on full-alert. Their bodies' tensed, willing to give in to the pre-programmed flight part of fight-or-flight.

The roo lay for a while, trying to figure out what happened, then untwisted its body, gave a little shake, bounded along, and up and over the next fence (by quite a margin), and disappeared. Our boys watched until the roo had completely gone. Their bodies were rigid beneath ours.

Noel and I stayed relaxed, keeping our voices soothing while we watched the rest of roos follow their mates. Eventually they were all gone, and the boys had no more excuses to stand and gawp.

We asked them to move forward, and on full-alert, we set off. Our team kept their heads high but soon released their tension and became supple once again.

As we settled into our rhythm we got lost. We walked up a hill and didn't understand what the map was showing us. We couldn't see another way. The boys stood and waited for us to work it out. Charlie fidgeted; he hated the delays, but eventually we came to an agreement, and he relaxed. We looked back down the hill and across a road and realised we should have turned right at the bottom. There were two gates: both were locked when we trekked passed. As we turned around to make our way back, we saw an official-looking van pull up near the gate. We legged on the horses – we didn't want to trot, the load was too clunky – but we didn't want to miss this guy either. I pushed on in front and yelled out.

'Hello, HELLOOOOO!' Luckily, he heard me and stopped. After we explained our navigation error, the park-ranger decided to help us.

'Yes, you have to go that way,' he said, pointing to the other side of the gates. 'I'll unlock the gates for you.'

'How would we have gone through this gate without you?' I asked. This particular gate had no other way around it!

'Don't start me,' he said as he untangled his keys. 'We have so many complaints about gates!'

'Well, you can add us to the list: that narrow walkway across the road, where we have to go, means we have to unload and load back up,' I said. 'It delays us, the boys are restless, and sometimes it is dangerous near busy roads.'

Our saviour agreed wholeheartedly. He told us about a large group ride that came through: they all had to unpack and re-pack, which took hours! We were so lucky to find him.

'There'll be more gates, I'm sorry to say,' he explained. 'I can't follow you to help you – sorry.'

We thanked him for his assistance. It had been a tremendous help. I continued to write a lengthy letter in my head to the powers-that-be.

The next set of narrow gates were slightly wider than usual, and we managed to squeeze through without unpacking. We were trekking through parkland now. No cars, no people, a few roos in the distance, but nothing bothering us. We were looking forward to stopping.

We figured we had another eight kilometres to go – we had to push on. The route took us through thicker wooded areas. Places where we could see a fire had ripped through at some point before us. It was a footpath you wouldn't want to traverse in the thick of summer, in a drought. The dead, dried timber was a fire waiting to happen. It had a beauty within its ugliness: bleached tangled timber, crunchy leaves, harsh, thick woodland, not friendly but somehow artistic.

We stopped in the tiny town of Tharwa; our guidebooks called it Cuppercumbalong. A small store gave us a moment's excitement: maybe we could buy some real food! Noel ventured inside to ask directions, just to make sure we were heading the right way.

'Here, enjoy.' Noel stepped out of the shop and handed me an ice-cream.

'Have they got lots of yummy things in here?' I asked as the frozen chocolate cracked and the ice-cream caused my taste buds to jump with joy.

'Erm, no, not really, it's a bit strange,' Noel said rather cryptically. 'But we only have about a kilometre to go before camp.'

'Great,' I said while trying to fight Charlie and Ned off. Those boys would eat anything.

We turned left into our new camp. Behind a shearing shed was a paddock made available for horses on the trail. It was a TSR with no water, but the property owners adjacent to the paddock allowed us use their tap and laundry room.

I was a bit dismayed with the lack of grass. It was tall and thin; I couldn't see much goodness in it. But they had a paddock with water buckets, and the paddock was on a hill, so the boys were relaxed and found enough to pick at.

Andrea, from Kangaroo Valley, was planning a visit. She had business to attend to in Canberra, and we were not that far from her appointment.

'It'll be great to see you!' I said on the phone, while explaining where we were.

'You too,' she agreed. 'What feed do you need?' I described a feed we had used previously.

'Basically anything that is high fat, full of goodies – cost doesn't matter.' I also asked her not to worry too much if she couldn't find exactly what I wanted. 'Just get what you can.' Andrea spent hours trying to find the best feed. I was so grateful and guilty; she knew just how important our boys were to us.

'Goodness you look exhausted and so skinny!'

'It's great to see you.' We all hugged, and then Andrea unloaded her car of freshly baked bread, ham, cheese, and home-baked cake. I drooled. I am a big eater, I love most foods, and quite often I will eat more than Noel. The days we were trekking, we'd usually have porridge for breakfast, and during the day we'd have half a Snickers bar and a handful of nuts. By the time evening was upon us we were so exhausted we'd only heat up a powdered soup or a cup of noodles. So when someone turned up with food it was exciting!

The three of us sat on the grass and talked about events in our lives. Andrea had become such a wonderful friend, always supportive, strong, and optimistic. Having the knack to turn any challenge into a positive was something I aspired to do.

'Anne sounds like a wonderful woman,' Andrea said when we'd detailed the help we had received.

'She is: you'd like each other; you're both strong women – she'll be here tomorrow.'

Anne had offered to take us shopping and drive us to the next camp. Not knowing what the following camp entailed was an extra challenge we didn't always enjoy. The guidebooks were good, but changes occur; fences could be down; was there grass? Water?

After lunch the three of us walked the boys down the road. There was a pretty creek surrounded with bright, clean sand. We thought the horses might like a play. We let them go, the three of us blocking the route back to the road. The boys weren't sure at first, but of course Dom rolled; he loved sand. They splashed and rolled and had a few minutes' fun. It was a relaxing interlude for us all.

All too soon Andrea left for her appointment; with us well fed and a huge bag of feed for the boys, we were set. Before she went, she drove us to the local shop.

I could see what Noel meant. The shop was caught in the forties: it was like a cave. The odd items of packaged food dotted the dark brown shelves, cunningly spread out to try to convince customers they weren't in a food drought. The fridge was packed with ice-creams; there was no cheese or ham. The bread was that horrid white, fluffy stuff, full of refined sugar. We managed to find a box of biscuits.

'You guys take care,' Andrea said as she squeezed me hard in a warm hug when she dropped us back.

'We'll be in touch when we can. Don't panic if you don't hear from us for a while – we don't always have a signal.'

While we did have a signal, we called family, checked emails, and tried to organise our gear. No matter how careful we were when we unpacked, we were always in a muddle, a constant battle of keeping our gear neat within the bags and having everything at hand. Every item we carried was used, but we couldn't leave everything out. Living out of bags was frustrating. I tried to colour coordinate, dark and light blue for kitchen items. My personal gear was in the burgundy bag, Noel's in the green. The rest was separated between the other bags. As the boys ate their food and we ate ours, the weight changed, and therefore the packing dynamics changed. Each bag had to be within a couple of grams of the opposite bag; each side had to bear the same weight, so we couldn't have the same items in the same bags; balance and distribution of weight was imperative.

Overnight the tent became covered in cicadas' outer shells. These fascinating creatures sing a shrill keening each evening at dusk, that amazing event when they all start together and all stop together. Female cicadas can also make a sound by flicking their wings, but it isn't the same as the male song cicadas are known for. Cicadas live in the ground for between two to seventeen years. When it is time for them to emerge, they climb up into the sun, which hardens their outer skin, this is shed, and they fly off. This is stated over-simply, but the outer shell is what we found on our tent, around our bags, along the fence, and up the tree. The shells are a little spidery (not my favourite creature), a couple of inches long and fascinating, with leg pieces too.

Anne arrived the next day, full of beans and ready to help.

'Right, where are we off to?'

'We'd love to check out the next campsite and maybe grab some provisions,' I said.

Caloola Farm was the next planned stop, about nineteen kilometres away.

'Great, let's go!' Anne said as she turned towards her car, and we gratefully sat on the soft seats and enjoyed the scenery flashing past without suffering sore bottoms!

'Aren't cars a marvellous thing?' Noel muttered to no-one in particular, and not for the first time.

19

Cheeky!

An afternoon chill settled on our shoulders, the wind sharpened, and rain threatened. The warning that weather could rapidly turn nasty in this area dangled in my mind. I was about to learn another lesson – check wet-weather gear *before* heading out!

The last five kilometres towards Caloola farm were all roadwork: a fast road that wasn't busy. Where it narrowed, we pushed the boys on; there was no verge, and cars passed us one at a time. We just had to get through this section. Storm clouds were approaching, which caused our legs to tighten around the boys to urge them forward. The ridge we'd been climbing flattened out, and a wide verge offered lush grass. We let the boys graze for a while. Huge gum trees stood like guarding sentinels watching us rest.

'I think we'd better rug up,' Noel said, peering at the thickening clouds.

A few drops of rain splashed on my knee; the bruised clouds indicated a soaking was imminent.

As we grappled with horses, gear, and clothing, a car pulled-up in front of us, thoughtfully allowing plenty of room. The passengers looked official.

'Hello, we're from National Parks.' A young couple grinned. 'Can we help?' They patted our boys and helped hold on to them while we dressed at the side of the road. Fortunately, the road was quiet, and any cars that turned up slowed down in kindness or curiosity.

'Where're you heading today? Caloola?'

'Yes, hopefully before we get too soaked!'

We all looked up at the sky and had the same thought, *nope – too late!*

'If you're continuing on the BNT, you'll need some codes,' said the woman. This made Noel stop, his leg dangling before he pushed it into his water-proof trousers.

'Codes?' He said shortly. 'Codes! I made several calls to your head-office about codes and was assured we would not need them!' He was laughing at this point, but I knew it was more hysteria than jovial. 'What's more, I called them back, twice no less, to double check!'

The couple looked at each other and muttered a comment about communication problems.

They handed us the codes, scribbled on a piece of paper, assuring us that we would need them over the next few days, after the next camp.

'Okay, are you sure they're right?'

'Yes, absolutely.'

'Sorry, to doubt you, but can you double check? We've already been misled: what if we are in the middle of nowhere without the right codes?' Noel said. He was becoming increasingly agitated.

The couple hesitated, but the guy pulled his mobile from a pocket and tapped out a number. 'Yes, they're the right codes, and you will be needing them.'

'That is all we'll need?'

'Yes, absolutely,' they said again. 'They're all the same for all the gates – you'll have no trouble.'

Noel started to calm, and we were both thankful that an 'accidental' meeting had been so fortuitous. After Caloola we would be trekking alone off-road; we didn't want to be stuck behind locked gates!

'Thanks so much, that's appreciated,' I said. Noel smiled his thanks too.

We were fully clad in wet-weather gear and hopped back on board. The wind commenced an evil howl. The couple climbed back in the car and drove off. The side-on driving wind and rain made the horses eager to turn their bottoms into it.

'There's something wrong with Stevie!' Noel called out to me.

Without looking around, I knew what was happening, for my boys were doing the same. 'It's the wind and rain – they want to turn their bottoms into it. Keep driving them on; we can't stop here.'

The temperature plummeted, the wind was biting, and the rain dropped heavily in plump lumps. My wet-weather jacket was as useful as a tissue. I was soaking wet and shivering.

We turned off the road and walked along farm trail-ways. A relief to be away from traffic, but now we had gates every five hundred metres. We couldn't walk around them for they were next to cattle grids or fencing; each gate had to be opened and closed. I could almost open a gate while on Charlie's back. A lot of people would think this is not such a great feat. But I had to hold Neddy, too, and Neddy didn't always pay attention when I was driving Charlie backwards. Also, Charlie was quite scared of a lot of things, and a big gate lurching toward him could make him reel in the opposite direction. So I had to be quiet, gentle, and slow. It wasn't possible with these gates, though, as the hinges were shot. The gates were nearly impossible to open from the ground, let alone a horse. We had to lift each hefty gate and carry it open. It was a struggle. The boys objected to the harsh weather, turning sideways and pulling on our arms while we heaved on the gate. The wind and rain had gathered momentum. Stinging water pellets battered us, the wind froze our skin, and the boys spun and fidgeted.

We opted to take it in turns. When you are icy cold and wet, the minutes turn into hours. At each gate one of us dismounted and handed our horses over to the other. The gate would be opened, horses collected and lead through, others ridden through. Horses back together, while the person on foot closed the gate again. We'd been riding for over four hours by this time, and we were stiff; our cold limbs complained. Both horses and riders were not happy.

We pushed on and on, endlessly. I was still shivering, so at least I hadn't reached hypothermia stage yet. It was serious though: I knew I was a prime candidate, and as well as monitoring the boys, I kept a close eye on my condition. Having been a sailor, I knew the dangers of losing body heat, but I didn't think I'd experience it on the trail!

We sighted the camp with relief. We knew we had shelter; we could build a fire; we could warm up, wash, and rest. We'd driven here previously, with Anne.

The manager, Geoff, had shown us where to camp saying, 'I'll just get my car keys and my .22 rifle!' Noel and I looked at each other. 'There are brown snakes down there where you'll be camping!'

The shelter was octagonal; we tied the boys to the poles and gained some welcomed protection too. With a system born from re-occurrence, we slung the gear under the refuge. There wasn't a need to create a corral; two square paddocks with neat timber fencing awaited the boys. The rain had stopped, but I still shivered. With swift work my muscles gradually warmed. Steam rose from the horses as we set them free in the paddock. They thrived on new abodes each night: they trotted to each corner, scrutinised, and snorted, while Noel and I scrubbed off the moss from their trough and re-filled it with clean water.

They drank clear cool liquid and enjoyed their freedom, stretching their backs, rolling in the dirt - their reward for carrying us here. Seeing them so happy was all the reward I needed.

'Right, now to sort us out,' said Noel. We both turned to our camp: it was messy, wet, and soggy. We had much work to do.

'How about we gather wood and light a fire, then tackle the tents,' I said.

'Good idea.'

We gathered sticks and logs into piles, in readiness to haul them back to camp. We were drying off, which made the tiredness easier to deal with. The thought of a warm fire propelled us on.

We lugged the piles of timber back to camp, and Noel worked his magic on a fire just outside the shelter.

I stood at the sink washing and looked at my hands and short, broken nails that were still muddy. 'I can't stand myself!' I said to Noel. 'Look!' I held up my hands. 'I can't stand the feel of my own hands – how can I not want to feel my own hands?'

'It won't last forever; we'll recover.'

I wasn't so sure. The next few days I stayed attached to the nail-file, but my nails were too short for it to be any use. My hands were dry and cracked, care of the biting wind.

With the fire crackling and exuding blissful yellow warmth, we unstacked plastic chairs and laid our gear over them, allowing it to dry: saddle blankets, saddles, bags, coats, everything. While it dried, we pitched the tents. I noticed the boys looking at me.

'You can wait,' Noel called out to them. They knew we had their dinner.

'Time to put us first for a bit,' said Noel, looking at all our equipment. I agreed – we were worn out and still a bit soggy. So we dragged out the camping gear and banged in tent pegs once again. With the fire crackling and the beds made, I could feed our boys.

They had wandered off but were instantly alert to the feed bags appearing. We divided up the sweet-smelling molasses, oats, and corns and pushed them all back from the gate. The thought of yummy food made them pushy, excited, and frantic not to be left out. Dom was young, impatient. Charlie was pretty awful too, so I fed him first. The others were a little calmer. Spirit was positively cool with the whole thing. His patience illustrated his intelligence: he knew he'd be fed; he didn't need to waste energy fretting.

They had dried off, so we buckled on their rugs while they ate. Satisfaction warmed my stomach, knowing the boys would stay warm and were filling their tummies with good food and clean water.

We waited while they ate. Some scarfed faster than others, then pestered the rest. Once they had finished, we unhooked their feedbags from their ears and shooed them away. With the boys settled for the night, we could cook our dinner. Noodles or soup were on the menu. Our tummies voiced empty rumbling. We were content with just having something to eat; it didn't matter what it was. Food had become a fuel and not a dining experience. Recipes were one-pot-wonders. The crackling fire filled the silence, and with full stomachs nestled within our canvas homes, we slept as soon as it was dark.

The sun chased away the wind and rain the following day. A bright clear morning greeted us, and our five boys were ensconced in the short but fertile grass. They didn't fret with the roos jumping around, a big improvement.

I splashed cold water on my face, scraped my dry knotted hair back into a ponytail, and cleaned my teeth beneath the twittering birds. With the ablutions done and dusted we tidied the camp and laid out the equipment in the sun. We indulged in the luxury of a sink with running water; I missed these simple things.

After filling up on thick porridge laced with brown sugar, we checked the adjoining paddock and opened up the gate to allow the team to wander further. They were content and glad to be left alone.

'I think I'll ring Anne,' I said to Noel as we sipped a restorative cup of tea. The sun was warming our backs; the air was fresh but warm. 'She did say if we needed any help...'

'I think that's a good idea; you can't continue without a waterproof jacket.'

Luckily we had mobile phone coverage. Anne knew where we were and was happy to come that same day.

'As long as we pay your petrol and take you to lunch,' I explained.

Warming under the sun we wrote a shopping list, including a sleeveless jacket for Noel to replace the one lost. Around lunchtime Anne arrived full of smiles and offering yummy cake. We spent a glorious afternoon together roaming through shops; the friendship between the three of us deepened.

Quickly we found some jackets that would do the trick. While I slipped on a red coat, Noel zipped up a navy blue.

'I'll get one too,' said Noel as he peered in the mirror.

'Good idea,' I agreed, 'but get red. I wouldn't be able to see you in the rain in that dark colour, so the drivers won't either – we need to be seen.' With that, we left the shop with two red jackets.

We lunched and sprinted around the supermarket buying more supplies and treats that we knew we wouldn't have to carry because we'd eat them before we left. We purchased meat for some protein and some chocolate and, of course, more noodles and soup.

Anne was reluctant to accept anything for helping us. But she had driven a fair way, so we made her take petrol money and a little more for a treat and a thank you. We don't expect something for nothing, and we were so grateful for her help. How else would we have done it?

Back at camp, our gear was drying nicely. The boys were fine.

'Do you think they need their rugs tonight?' asked Noel.

'I'm not sure. I feel inclined to put them on as it can drop, but they may be okay.' I thought for a while. I worried that if the temperature plummeted during the night, they'd drop weight quickly. 'We'll put them on.' Noel was doubtful they needed them, but it made me feel better!

Dom, Stevie, and Spirit accepted their rugs without a problem. We had already fed them, leaving their rugs for the last thing before dark, as the day had warmed up so much.

Charlie made a fuss – he walked off and messed about, but I strapped his rug on. I should have taken the hint. Neddy was the last to do. He looked at me, and I looked at him. I carried his rug towards him.

'Come on, Neddy-boy, time for your PJs.' He walked off. I tried to step in front of him; he trotted off. The others started joining in with the game too.

'Neddy, naughty Neddy,' I called, giggling. Ned trotted past me as if teasing. He looked back and did a little buck in my direction – the other horses following. I swear, he laughed – he certainly had a big grin on his face. It was one big joke to him. He didn't want his rug on, and he was letting me know and being cheeky at the same time.

I laughed. 'I don't think Ned wants his rug on tonight, fair enough!'

The sight of Ned playing, having a game, and even being a bit cheeky with the little buck in my direction (as if to say 'nerr ner na na nerr!') was pure delight. Ned hadn't had an easy life: his nerves had been handled with impatience, creating a vicious circle making him worse. He can't have had much affection. If you raised your voice or a hand he quivered – literally. And all he wanted to do was please. He had become so relaxed and trusting with us, that now he could be cheeky, he could have a joke, some fun, and not fear being reprimanded. The look on his face that day will stay with me forever and brings a tear every time I think of it. If you've ever seen delight, freedom, love, kindness, and gratitude in an animal's face you'll understand.

The following night, we left all their rugs off. It was warm enough, so I had to stop worrying.

After a few days' rest, it was time to set off. The next part was off-road. We'd be reading maps and trying to follow the yellow BNT signs. We were heading for Horse Gully Hut.

We paid our dues at the office (about five dollars per night) and thanked them for providing such a lovely, private, safe spot.

The trail led us out the back of the property, through rusting gates and into tangles of bush. We'd been on the move less than an hour, and after climbing a small hill, Dom's pack had already slipped. We stopped, tied the boys to trees, and re-packed Dom from the start. I don't know why this kept happening. We did the same thing each day. We took extraordinary care, but some days it just didn't work. This always made the situation a bit tense. We had miles to cover: we couldn't afford to lose too much time. And then we'd worry about the packs the rest of the way. However, both Noel and I were trying not to direct our frustrations at each other. I noticed we both bit our tongues, not allowing comments, advice, and those destructive long sighs to hinder the situation further. We were learning not to act on our emotions all the time.

The gum trees fought for supremacy against the scrub along this part of the trail. There was no opportunity to let the boys have a feed along the way, and we kept thinking there would be food at the next stop. We reached the first coded gate, and the magic numbers released the lock. We walked along deserted paddocks, up bridleways and down hills, turning onto a scrubby course-way. Dead trees reached across the path, and not one sprout of life could be seen. Twisted, ugly branches hung in death: an insect infestation had caused a holocaust throughout this forest. Enormous branches dangled around us, clinging on with barely a splinter. The wind gathered momentum, completing the horror movie scene. I wondered how long it would be before a tree fell and caused havoc within our troop. Silent and foreboding as this stretch was, we were glad it wasn't fire season just yet. A small spark and this area was ready to go up in a towering inferno.

Apparently, we crossed a river eight times in this section. We splashed through a few small creeks, but mostly it flowed beneath the packed mud, unseen. Eventually, we witnessed the start of tenacious new life, fighting through the moon-scape grey, making a slow but forceful green comeback via the odd pink flower. This was the first time we had no cars to worry about for most of the day, and it was a great relief. We started to enjoy the trail.

Horse Gully Hut

Along the narrow, tree-lined track, the pathway opened up to reveal a small corrugated iron hut on our left. There was a useful hitching post, too, and a clearing with good grass. We had only ridden for four hours. We tied up, unpacked, and constructed the corral. Surrounded by forest, the silence rose between the mobs of chewing kangaroos. The boys were alert but not unduly concerned.

With the horses in their paddock, the temperature dropped, so we unfolded the rugs. Ned trotted toward me when he saw what we were doing. I am sure he was grinning. Just the opposite to the cheeky antics he displayed when he didn't want the blanket. It was as if he could see the funny side of it too.

We hauled our gear into the comfy hut. There was a rain-water tank, filled via the roof. The boys were waiting for the buckets and took long deep swallows, then settled down to eat. We made camp indoors, grateful that it wasn't necessary to pitch tents. We lit the fire and luxuriated on the old timber chairs next to a table. We tried to keep fairly organised, as we were only staying one night. With all of us fed, we slept well; there was no remaining energy to think about being in the middle of nowhere.

We were up early and tied the boys to the post near the rail. It took the usual several hours to pack them up, but this time we had some extra fun. The kangaroos kept running at us. One in particular was so fascinated with our troop, he'd hop straight toward the boys. It was as if he was saying, *Watch this fellas, see how I can make these big horses panic.*

As he closed in, they became agitated, unhappy they were tied up and couldn't move away. Up until now the roos had hopped away from them, not towards them. We were trying to saddle and pack the boys, and they were swinging around trying to face the roo. Armed with a stick, I shooed the cheeky marsupial away. But the boys were tetchy and restless.

As we strapped on the last of the gear, we talked about swapping horses.

'I'd like to ride Ned for a change,' Noel said, stroking his neck.

'Good idea, I don't mind who I ride or lead, but don't tie Spirit to your saddle. Ned can be unpredictable.'

'He'll be okay – we're safe here.' I didn't like this, but Noel was a good rider and making his own decisions. And he was right: Ned had been so good, just leading along without a drama for a few weeks now.

I continued to ride Charlie, as we couldn't pack him with much. So Stevie was packed this time, together with Dom and Spirit.

We let Dom go, thinking he'd just follow, and set off. I was leading Stevie. Dom followed for a few steps then stopped to eat. I thought he'd munch for a bit, fall behind, and catch up. But Dom had other ideas. He stopped eating, caught up with us, but when he reached the group, he turned around and headed in the other direction! I had no idea what he was thinking.

'Dom, Dommiiieeeeee,' we both called.

'Keep going, he'll come,' I said, looking back.

We kept walking, and then we heard Dom call. He didn't come back: he just bellowed!

'Good grief,' I said. 'It doesn't look like he's coming back; now he's fretting as he can't see us!' We had stopped at this point.

Ned became fidgety, and something made him jump. He didn't like the group being broken up either, or being away from Charlie's side. He swung around; Spirit was fantastic at being led, but he wasn't ready for Ned's quick movement, nor was Noel.

Spirit's lead rope was suddenly across Noel's crotch, about to swipe him clean off Ned. With quick, clear thinking, born from a survival gene, Noel leaned back and flipped the rope up and over his head. It was so close to being a disaster. He told Ned off. Fear being emotion, anger being the result.

I offered to lead Dom and Spirit, leaving Noel to lead Stevie. He could let Stevie go if he had to, if Ned played up. He didn't tie Stevie to his saddle.

'It's dangerous, tying anything to Ned!' Noel muttered.

I managed to avoid saying, 'I told you so.'

'You could ride Charlie one day,' I suggested. 'I'd like to ride Ned or one of the others.'

Noel looked at me dubiously. 'We'll see.' He wasn't sure of Charlie. I could understand why – he was a bit unpredictable. But he was improving each day. When he was striding out in confidence, he was a real power horse. He was so joyful, but you had to be ready. If something made him jump, he was off like a shot!

Soon we arrived at Mount Clear, and I was horrified that there was no grass. We hardly had any feed, and the boys were hungry. Along the way we had stopped a couple of times to let them munch for five or ten minutes; it was good grass, but it wasn't enough. The paddock was large but bare. There were two horses already trying to graze, their owners packing up from a night's stay. We kept our boys tied up until they had loaded theirs into the trailer. They had a surplus of hay and feed and were heading home to more.

'Can I buy some feed from you, please?' I asked. 'Just tell me what you want for it – I'll take hay too, as much as you can spare.'

For twenty dollars we purchased half a bale of hay and enough feed for a good dinner for the boys that night and some breakfast. It wasn't enough, but it'd help.

However, the lady repeatedly delved back into the supplies she had sold to me, as she didn't think her boy had enough. Her horse was well cared for and obviously loved, but he'd be home in a few hours with as much food as he wanted. We had nothing else. I was upset and annoyed, not with the cost, but the food was dwindling. While unloading our boys, I moved the precious food nearer to us, hoping she'd get the hint.

Alone, the horses wandered around the paddock. They didn't stop to eat, for there was nothing to eat. The worry of lack of food caused my tummy to flip.

We set up our camp and put the fence around us, so they couldn't intrude around the tents; I knew they would try. They stood at the fence looking into our camp with forlorn faces. I set off on a walk; we had the afternoon free, and I had had a brief rest, and searching for grass seemed a good idea, but there was nothing nearby.

Noel was dozing just outside our camp. I was trying to rest but was agitated about food; there was nothing I could do, or was there? Spirit and Dom nuzzled Noel – he had fallen asleep but was woken by four nostrils of warm breath. They nuzzled him and prodded him, no doubt searching for food. They were so gentle, eight big hooves near his head. The trust Noel had with these two enormous beasts, millimetres away from crushing him, was beautiful to witness. I indulged in the satisfaction of helping create that trust and our fierce bonds – emotions that were altogether wonderful and worrisome – this was my family.

Oats, the thought of oats came into my head. We carried a lot of porridge. It's a great food, easy to make and filling. Aside from noodles and soup, this was our main diet. We had stocked up on oats, and I dug them out of our packs.

We had about eight small packets; it would only be a few mouthfuls each, but something more to give them. That evening I divided up the feed we had purchased and saved the oats. We scattered the hay around the paddock, but with five big hungry boys, it was only a few mouthfuls each. They finished their dinner and watched us eat. I had to turn my back on them.

The following morning I gave them the oats. Noel smiled at me and rolled his eyes. They loved them. They then drank, and I hoped that the oats would swell in their stomachs and satisfy them a little while we packed up. We would have stayed another day, but we needed grass. Horses eat a lot and for about ninety percent of the day. Everything they do expels energy. When they walk around to eat, this uses energy, which they have to replace.

Noel wanted to ride Stevie. It was a tried and tested set-up and safer. Noel had a new appreciation for Stevie's bravery and assuredness. Ned wasn't too happy to be carrying again. He pulled his ears back a few times, not in nastiness, but in questioning. *Am I okay?* you could almost hear him ask. With plenty of pats and reassurance, he settled down and relaxed.

We were heading for Bradleys Creek. It wasn't a designated stop. The official camp site at Yaouk was thirty kilometres away, too much for us in one day. I prayed that we would find grass for the boys along the way.

There wasn't a car, a person, or anything else to worry about. The boys knew they were safe – we were in the company of nature, and it was superbly peaceful. Noel started to sing, a sure sign he was relaxed and enjoying himself.

Was this it? I thought. *Now that we've worked it out, will it run smoothly from here on?* I hoped so. The packing up for hours each morning was tiring, but this morning's packing appeared easier. It had taken just as long. Perhaps we had finally scaled the difficult hump – maybe.

As we trekked along I tried to grasp what it was that I liked so much 'out here.' It was a little like sailing on oceans: natural, no forced pathways, no man-made walls; the bush rules; the ocean rules; nothing was forced or fake. It was real, inviting, calming, and received my complete respect.

Along the way we found fabulously rich grass, and the boys' jaws ground gratefully on the lush green strands. We dismounted, allowing them to roam for a good twenty minutes. I kept hold of Charlie, knowing Ned wouldn't wander too far. Noel stayed with Stevie, leaving Spirit and Dom attached. They'd learned not to waste time and quickly filled with food while they could. We were tucked amid a dense forest, but for the first time the boys didn't worry about predators, they were so hungry. With our limbs stretched, Noel and I indulged in standing upright.

Charlie had suffered a minor rub on his heel, so he sported a bandage to protect it. It was probably from a small stone that flicked in, as his boots didn't rub him usually, but they would rub against this sore. He didn't like the bandage, and it was tricky to keep in place, but he needed protection. While he was munching, I re-adjusted the dressing; his wound wasn't any redder, so my handiwork was working.

Reluctantly, we gently hauled on their heads and walked them over to a steady incline, making the effort of mounting easier, and carried on. After a shaky start, I was starting to feel a little fondness for the BNT. The hard busy roads had been replaced with soft peaceful trails; this was now home, and opening up to reveal its unique splendour.

The sound of hooves padding along springy grass and squeaking leather accompanied us down a small slope, where we reached a bulky timber gate, bound with a hefty chain and a number lock. We had the code to hand, and I held Stevie, Spirit, and Dom while Noel tried the lock. The fence stretched away and down from the entrance for miles. Beyond the gate was a dirt road, then another fat, gated paddock with more locks to undo. It was deserted; an incongruous mix of infinite meadows and snarly scrub surrounded the yellow dirt road, and blue sky unfolded above us for miles. The peaceful moment was suddenly shattered.

'*Shit*, bugger, *fuck*!' I heard. 'You bloody bastards, you stupid, effing, bloody bastards!'

I knew we were in trouble.

'The code isn't working!' Noel carried on with his colourful string of harsh words that continued on to include all the national parks' employees, their line of work, and quite a few of their family members!

'Shall I have a go?' I offered, while Noel filled his lungs for the next barrage.

Noel stomped back to the horses, muttering angrily, and I tried the gate.

'I don't believe it, those idiots: have we got a signal?'

We tied the horses to a fence and dug out the phones from the saddle-bags. No signal.

'Christ almighty, now what?' Noel asked.

'Look, there's a car coming – let me see if I can find some help.' I leaped over the fence and flagged down the car.

'Excuse me, we are stuck; we can't open the gates. I need to call someone. Could I pay to use your phone?' The man was happy for me to try to attempt a call, but he had no signal either – we weren't his problem, and he shrugged his shoulders and drove off, leaving me in a swirling dust cloud.

The boys knew there was something wrong; they were in tune with our moods. We were well and truly stuck.

I inspected the fence. 'Hey, Noel, someone has already cut this fence and twisted it back together here; maybe we could undo it?'

Noel searched for his Leatherman tool, meanwhile muttering, 'And the idiots that manage the parks wonder why people do it, how could they mess this up so spectacularly, I called them three times, we met them in the road, they even checked the numbers, good grief, what a sham!'

Fortunately, the small tool was up to the job, and he snipped at the fence and unravelled the springy wires. We tied the boys up to the secure gate. It took half an hour to pull back a stretch of fence wide enough for the troop and their packs. We had to do the same just a few strides across the road.

With both fences open, Noel and I led Stevie, Spirit, and Dom through together carefully. One at a time, I tied them up on the other side and traipsed back for Charlie and Ned. They had been watching us. Charlie only speaks when there is food. But as he saw me return, he whickered softly. His call said so much: he thought we were going to leave him; the relief in his little call brought tears to my eyes. I gave him a hug and a good pat, Ned too.

'I'll never leave you boys; I'll never let you down.'

Words I would have to swallow later on while my heart broke.

Noel had tied up the other three, and he helped me with Charlie and Ned. They still didn't like narrow spaces, and we didn't need them hooked up on a fence. We tied them together on the second gate, and while we twisted the fences back together, I was already composing a letter.

Flailing Limbs

The hour-long delay was soon forgotten, and we settled into a pleasurable ride. Thick wooded expanses ran alongside us. Up and down hills, we trekked with only the trees and leaves for company, not a soul to be seen. Birds hooted, and critters scampered away from our large troop. The boys were glistening, their muscles rippling. Noel and I were sinewy. Our rescued family had become confident, strong, brave. They knew at the end of the day we would find safe grazing for them, where they could rest, be rugged up, fed, watered, and relax, in the company of the team. They were fit, and if the day was easy and uneventful, they'd become silly, burning up excess energy. They'd shy at their own shadows on occasions; I'm sure they winked at each other before doing so. But so many days were eventful, there was never a dull moment, and we were just longing for one boring day.

At the bottom of a small gully, we trekked past a large spread of majestic rocks.

'Can we get a picture?' I had carried the camera in my saddle-bags, but it was a pain to pull it out. We hadn't taken many pictures, so it was time to stop, take time, and dig out the camera. The delay with the fence wasn't too bad, as we were splitting the thirty kilometre journey into two. I passed Noel the camera. He had dismounted and was holding Stevie; Spirit and Dom waited patiently while Noel snapped off some shots.

As Noel handed the camera back to me (I was still on Charlie), Dom's lead rope became caught around Spirit's back leg. It was me that had tied it on, and I'd left it just that tiny bit too long. I had used the wrong line too. Such a simple little thing was about to cause mayhem.

Spirit was the cool dude amongst the group, but even this was too much for him. As Dom raised his head, he pulled Spirit's back-leg up. Spirit did not like this and forced his leg down, taking Dom's head with it. Dom didn't like this. Between them, they panicked and ran around in circles with Dom's head up, then down, with Spirit's leg working in opposition, like a crazy clockwork toy. Of course, Spirit was still tied to Stevie, who hadn't a clue what was going on, but wasn't too happy being attached to this bizarre dance. He was shoved forward and dragged backwards, so he joined in with the melee. Noel was trying to grab Stevie's head to stop him, then tried to grab hold of anything; he needed to release the line. It was becoming more and more frantic as nodding heads and flailing limbs twisted into tighter and tighter circles. I leaped off Charlie to help, but I daren't let my two go. I had to tie them up first, which seemed to take forever. I left them with a small plea to 'just stand.'

As I grabbed Spirit, Noel released the line around Spirit's leg, and everything stopped. We didn't know who helped who, but finally the merry-go-round had ceased.

We all stood together, big breaths, heaving stomachs, and wide eyes.

Spirit seemed to say, *For goodness sake, what took you so long to get me out of that mess?*

Dom said, *I dunno what happened there, but it was kinda fun.*

Meanwhile, Stevie said, *What the hell was that all about?*

Noel and I were asking ourselves the same questions: we agreed with them all, except the bit Dom might have said.

Dom suffered no injuries; Spirit had a couple of grazes, but that was all. Noel and I had a good few more grey hairs and plenty of adrenaline stampeding around our bodies. Stevie's ruffled feathers were now back in place. We sorted out the lines and put the right lead rope in the correct place and tested its length. It was important that the horse being led could only just reach the grass by the back feet of the one it was tethered to. The line must not be loose. I took such care with everything when I packed, but just an inch of extra line caused a problem. We couldn't relax about anything for one moment.

Again we spent a few minutes calming the boys, reassuring. It helped us calm too. I apologised to them, for it was all my fault. I could see Spirit look at me as if to say, *Yeah, I knew it was you.*

We mounted up and started off again. I was always amazed how quickly we settled back into a good pace. We all stepped into our rhythm as though nothing had happened. We could admire the views, breathe in the earthy scents, and simply enjoy the steady meandering through a marvellously diverse country. All was well, until the next hill.

'Spirit's saddle blanket is slipping.' Noel scowled.

'We have to adjust it,' I said, asking my boys to stop. 'You hold them – I'll sort it.'

Time was marching on as we had now suffered so many delays. The woods became thicker but starker. Dead gum trees had fallen; those that hadn't were dry, ready to topple. The wind was picking up, and I was waiting for a tree to fall across our path or worse, on or near us! I was tense but trying to relish the unique panorama, the silence, the whispering winds, timelessness.

As we approached the next gate, we knew it'd be another problem. We tried the numbers, and they didn't work, so we offered up a few more colourful words saved especially for these moments. However, we then spotted the mangled fence, right next to the gate, a little hidden by growth. It looked as though it had been down a while. The gate was brand new; it must have cost thousands, and next to it the fence was falling apart and knocked down!

We tied the boys to the sturdy gate and cleared more fence so there was no chance of a tangle. Without hesitation, the boys ducked under the growth and stepped over strands of wire that we held down with our feet. They pivoted on their hooves while negotiating these hurdles and squeezed through the narrow gap. One at a time, they calmly trusted us and walked through. After the dramas of the day, our adrenaline had sapped our energy dry. Heavy weariness caused our limbs to sag. The boys sensed that there was no need for dramas.

What was supposed to feel like a short day had now become epic. Time had stretched away from us. We had one and a half kilometres to go; the wind was howling and making the going more arduous than it should have been.

'How far to go now?' I asked, while Noel consulted the GPS.

'A kilometre.'

'What, still?'

'I'm afraid so,' he said, double-checking his calculations.

We still didn't know where we were camping that evening. The map had promised a creek near a paddock. This spot was a gamble; it wasn't listed as a campsite. *Would we be able to access the paddocks or the creek?* The next 'advised' stop would add another ten kilometres to the trip. That was not the popular choice: we'd just make it if there were no further problems, but our muscles were already complaining.

Part-way we had to adjust packs again: Spirit's had moved, and Noel became agitated. There was nowhere to tie the boys up, and nothing to eat, so they became restless.

Noel and I sniped at each other.

'It just has to be done.'

'I know, but it's a pain in the arse!'

'Well, there's no point griping about it; we just need to get the job done and carry on.'

'I know, but I can gripe if I want to!'

We weren't angry with each other, or the horses. It was just tiredness and probably fear. We'd had a frustrating day, and we'd both kept our cool – we do in fraught conditions when we just have to deal with what's going on, not bicker about it. But it felt as though the packs were in control of us. We had to ensure they were absolutely right. The boys relied on us. We'd already messed up with Dom. At this point of the day, the pains started to clutch at our bodies – our bottoms and legs ached. My toes were numb. Noel's knees throbbed. We tried walking, but the boys strode out so fast it was hard to keep up with them. If something made them jump, they lurched forward, whether we were there or not. Even if they swerved around us, their packs would have knocked us flat. We had better visibility and control whilst riding, and we didn't have to intuit the invisible so much.

The track ceased, and we turned right onto a road, and so it was back to road work. It was late; we were all ready to stop.

The map indicated we were close to the area we hoped to rest. I eyed the verges sceptically. *Could we squeeze them in there?* I wondered, but it was right by the road! We'd have to do shifts all night to ensure they didn't break out. I could feel my shoulders tightening and my forehead creasing.

As I was looking down onto an open paddock thinking, *We could trek over that hill and hide in the corner,* a car pulled up. Paul stepped out with his young horse groom, Jane.

'I remember you from the pack-saddle workshop,' said Noel.

Paul smiled. 'I knew you'd turn up eventually. My place isn't that far away. You'd make it today, and you'd be welcome.'

'Thanks so much.' I pointed to the field. 'Could we stop there?' I asked hopefully.

'Go for it; I know who owns it,' he said. 'He won't know you are there; watch the fences though, he doesn't fix them - you'll be fine,' he explained further. 'Tomorrow you'll reach my place. I have a paddock and shed for you to stay in.'

'Thanks so much – that'd be great. We'll stay here for tonight at least, maybe two nights; then we'll come along.'

'Whenever you like – see you soon.' He and Jane waved and drove off, kicking yellow dust into the air.

With some relief, we found the gate open a few metres further on; the boys had a keen sense of a change: we were off the road, heading into a rich green paddock with lots of yummy grass. Suddenly Charlie shot off, and Ned's head jerked forward before I let him go.

'Whoa, whoa, steady.' I glanced around wondering if I'd have to ditch. Paul's advice to watch for wires was still lurking in my head. I thought Charlie had become entangled in something I hadn't seen, and he'd panicked.

As quickly as it all started, he stopped. Ned's rope had slid under his tail again. I'd have to watch for that all the time. He instantly flew into a mad panic and clamped his tail onto the rope – if only he'd relax, the rope wouldn't burn! I tried to explain this to him, but he wouldn't listen.

We carefully trekked our way down to the bottom of the hill, the boys with a spring in their step; they knew their day was almost done. The creek at the foot was inviting, but we'd learned to pick our camp spot first, so we didn't have to carry our heavy supplies too far. The trouble was, there were no trees on our side of the creek. Somehow we had to hold the boys.

'We'll have to hobble them,' said Noel.

'Okay.' I hated hobbles, just detested them. It was like putting our boys in hand-cuffs. The journey was about freedom. I didn't want to, but we had no choice. The hobbles were homemade, and we hadn't practiced with them enough. I was so soft: I hated seeing the boys stumble. I recalled Charlie's first time in hobbles at Kangaroo Valley. He became theatrical beyond imagination and sulked. He refused to eat and stood there glaring at me until I took them off. Then I remembered how Noel had glared at me for being so soft. Charlie had me well and truly wrapped up around his hoof right from the start.

Now, I was too tired to worry about Charlie's feelings, so I hauled out the hobbles from the saddle-bag, and we strapped them on.

We let Dom go, thinking he'd just eat. We set to unpacking the other boys, each of us holding two horses while unsaddling. It wasn't easy, as they were desperate to eat.

We were tired; unpacking was slow and heavy. Our legs ached, and we had several hours of work in front of us.

Suddenly Noel yelled, 'DOM!'

I looked around, and Dom had staggered over to the creek. He was still fully loaded. I gave my boys to Noel and trotted over to him. As I was almost upon him, he stepped into the creek, the mud slithered up to his knees. He couldn't separate his front legs so he fell forward.

'Christ! HELP!' I yelled. But Noel was busy hanging onto the other four.

I waded in, knowing I was in danger, if Dom panicked I'd end up under him. But that didn't stop me. I grabbed his head and tugged his nose out of the water so he didn't drown. He tried to haul himself back. Somehow, I scrambled under his neck and pushed like an adrenaline-crazed lunatic. As I slid down further into the water, he rose up and, with a huge lurch, heaved himself back onto hard land.

'You fucking idiot!' I said, and he looked at me. I said it gently for I had no breath or energy left. The adrenaline was making its exit. Those words were directed at me, not at Dom: he was just thirsty. Dom and I staggered back to the troop.

'The hobbles aren't working; they're too loose. We should have done more training with them,' said Noel through gritted teeth, his anger derived from the fear of watching Dom and I almost drown.

'I *know*!' I yelled, acutely aware and sickened that not only was I under-prepared, I wasn't capable of looking after us all. Noel and I continued to bicker while unpacking the horses. This arguing was so odd; we'd witnessed other couples bicker like this, and usually we didn't do it. It wasn't weighing on our minds too much – we knew that it was pent-up fear needing to be released. It wasn't nasty, just tired niggles, but it still wasn't healthy.

Finally, the boys were free, and we constructed the paddock. The lush grass held their attention while we banged in posts and looped on the electric wire. The corner of the paddock included the creek, so the boys had their fill. They stood on thick grass, and they knew dinner would be served soon and we'd leave them alone. They'd fulfilled their part of the bargain.

Noel and I then turned to pitching our tents. We weren't talking now, so our tents were not close. We both soon tired of these petty niggles and had decided it was better to say nothing. We worked on the tasks at hand, moved our tents nearer, and made a comfortable camp.

'We're tucked in nicely with plenty of food, shelter and privacy,' said Noel looking around, leaning on the pile of backpacks.

'Mmmm, are you thinking of staying another day?'

'Why not? We could all do with a rest; this is a great paddock.'

I looked about, feeling a little uneasy that we were on someone's land uninvited.

Noel noticed.

'Look, this hasn't been used for ages; there are no weeds, no cow poo, no fences. No one's coming here – no one would care. Worst case is, we move tomorrow.'

'You're right,' I agreed, and started to relax.

I made up the feeds, and the boys walked over to the fence, eagerly awaiting their food. With their bags on, we hung around so they didn't bother each other. Charlie was a menace: he'd bolt his food then try to eat the others'. With their stomachs full, they wandered off, munching the lush grass. Horses are wanderers; it's what they do naturally, and they were doing that, albeit with us. They thrived on it. The routine suited them; they had also changed. They were all solid, fit, with strong, large muscles bulging beneath shiny coats. Just looking at them gave me a depth of fulfilment that made my stomach flip.

Noel and I ate our obligatory noodles and settled into bed. I barely had the energy to take my socks off. It was nice to know we weren't getting up at first light.

'G'night, pettley-pie,' Noel called out. 'I love you.'

'I love you too, squirrel-head.'

We both chuckled. I swallowed some pain-killers and fell into an exhausted sleep.

The next day, after breakfast, we moved the paddock over so they could chew down fresh grass. We carried out repairs and cleaning and took it easy. We discussed the packing, constantly trying to find solutions to make it easier, especially when we had nothing to tie the boys to. We agreed that one of us should have held all the boys while the other unpacked; it was as easy as that. It all makes sense when you've had a rest.

Strong Bones

The following day we were back on the road. We had only half a day's jaunt. We were glad we stopped where we had, as it was another three hours to Paul's place.

From Bradleys Creek the smooth tarmac road changed into a dirt track, though it was still used by cars, for it was the only route to use in this area. The ugly twisted scrub that accompanied this section hung dry and listless. Makeshift homes and dirty caravans dotted between the grey trees. *Bush fire heaven* was all I could think. Scrubby vistas with struggling growth from poor soil and lack of rain tangled skyward, where the vibrant blue tried to penetrate and relieve the bland colours.

We reached vast plains with little traffic, and the dry scrub morphed into lush greens infused with yellows that seemed to light up the paddocks. Dainty sun-yellow flowers became a shimmering sheet of colour that escorted us for several kilometres. The vibrancy of life, a stark comparison from just an hour before; the sharpening of the blues and greens with the bright flowers made a dazzling collage of zest and bite.

The boys walked fast, keen to see what would happen next. Noel and I changed the lead, swapping the camera, taking shots. The boys powered on with clear eyes and heads held high – we had a good day. Better because it was shorter. We knew where we were going. The peaceful ride allowed me to reflect on where I was going, not the location, but my life. Did I have a destination? Maybe I'd already arrived. Perhaps my place was not a physical site but a person and horses. I'd not had a long term plan; I still don't. But with all the unexpected twists and turns of this escapade, it made me look forward to the future to new and exciting horizons.

Over the brow of the hill we spotted Paul's place. As we strode down the quiet road a mare and foal trotted over in greeting. A gorgeous little foal all fluff and legs: it couldn't have been more than a year old. The boys were fascinated, but not as much as me. I love little foals. This one held no fear; it ran right to the fence.

Without warning Charlie suddenly spun around and darted across the road. In an instant I knew the lead rope was stuck under his tail. All I could think about was pulling it out, and as he hesitated half-way across the road, I thought I'd leap off and retrieve the rope. A daft, stupid notion. By the time my brain clicked into realising how idiotic this idea was, I was half-way off. Charlie had then figured out where he was going and swerved to the right. This forced me forward and down. With a sickening thud, I met the bank that rose abruptly into, what felt like, a solid wall.

The air was punched out from my lungs. Head to toe pain throbbed in a numbing way. The jolt of impact flowed through to the tips of my teeth and finger nails. I was starkly reminded that I was no longer in my twenties.

'Christ almighty, are you okay? Jack, JACK!' I could hear panic in Noel's voice.

When I had come off before (this was becoming a habit I would have to kick!) I usually bounced straight back up to grab Charlie and a piece of dignity. But I couldn't this time. I couldn't speak or move. I was scared to move; I thought I had damaged something.

'I'm okay,' I croaked eventually, lying through my teeth. 'Get Charlie; where's Ned?'

'They're okay,' Noel said through his clenched jaw. What he meant was, *I don't care about them* – he was angry with me, angry with them. Fear's such a complex emotion.

I gradually moved bit by bit.

189

'Ohhh, there's going to be some pretty colours on me tomorrow.' I grinned.

'What on earth were you doing? You were sitting nicely on him – why did you try to get off?'

'I thought... I thought it was the right thing, I dunno, it was stupid, just stupid, a split-second decision, which was dumb. I thought I could get the rope out,' I finished weakly.

'It would have slid out soon enough – you have to start thinking of you and not the boys. They are big enough to deal with this; these are mere scratches to them!' He took a breath. 'I thought you'd really hurt yourself then.'

'So did I,' I said meekly, laying still without shifting, hoping Noel hadn't noticed my lack of movement.

'You need to thank your mum!'

I looked at Noel; my head was starting to pound.

'What on earth has my mum got to do with this?'

'All those good dinners she made you – you have strong bones; if you hadn't you would have broken at least six just then. You are so strong, and it's your mum's doing!' He was almost shouting at me.

Noel was right: I could have easily broken something, and by rights I should have; irreparable damage with a broken back or neck could happen so easily. The bank had shaken with my collision. It was like hitting a brick wall at thirty miles an hour. I knew I'd be stiff for a few days, but my toes and fingers wriggled without causing much pain, so I knew I'd recover.

'I reckon you shook a couple of buildings on the other side of the planet with that impact,' Noel muttered as he stomped off to retrieve Charlie and Ned.

I looked around from my now comfortable position on the ground. Paul's house was high up, to our right; as the large paddocks swept up to a copse of trees, the house sat tucked in between them. I scanned back down to the sheds and paddocks opposite the mare and foal, just fifty metres away. No one was around. I was relieved.

I lay quietly while Noel reunited the boys. I wondered why I hadn't broken any bones. I had drunk a lot of milk in my youth. Spending endless summer nights with my ponies, becoming hot and sweaty, I'd sneak in the kitchen and gulp down a complete pint of cold, full-cream milk. I smiled to myself remembering infants' school, when we all were made to drink small bottles of milk every day. My mates hated it; I loved it. They were forced to drink it, so when the teacher's back was turned, I'd systematically swap empty bottles for full ones.

Noel returned with Charlie. 'Don't tell them what happened,' I said, glancing at the house in the distance. 'I could do without judgement, or worse, sympathy.'

In truth, I was feeling stupid. When we'd discussed taking on this trekking escapade, I had laughingly told Noel, 'You're not considered a rider until you've fallen off at least eight times.'

He hadn't been that chuffed with that idea. It was what I had grown up with. I had fallen off countless times over the years. Still, I was smug at the start of this trip. I knew Noel would fall off quite a few times and I probably wouldn't; I had great balance usually. Now, I was eating humble pie in rather large portions. Noel had rolled off the back of Ned once at Kangaroo Valley, just losing his balance while mounting. Meanwhile, I had suffered two heavy falls. It was embarrassing and shaking my already crumbling confidence in my ability to make this work.

Paul and his helper Jane made us welcome. They gave the boys a paddock with water and plenty of grass. We didn't have to put up our fence. They offered us the shed with running water, table, and chairs. We stayed a few days, and Paul loaned us his run-about car, so we took advantage and took a trip to suss out the next camp and arrange horse feed. The food we carried was so bulky and heavy, it would be nice to have it already organised further along.

The next day I was stiff, but not too bad considering. I wandered over to see the mare and foal across the road. Paul explained that the mare wasn't the natural mum. They'd found the foal abandoned, half-dead in the wild, while trekking. They'd brought it back, and this mare had mothered the darling little creature. It was a filly and a real feisty girl. She was tough and wanted to play. She nipped, skipped, hid, and galloped and leaped, and I did the same, ignoring my pains. This foal thought itself human or me a foal. Mum was shy but stood by as the foal and I played the fool. What a marvellous little creature: she'd steal someone's heart and then rule them completely, a tough filly, destined for a great life.

Going to the loo was a pain here. I had to be completely private, which meant traversing the foal's paddock and climbing up a hill to some bushes. At least I had an excuse to play with the foal each day. Our diet of little meat – mainly Snickers bars and noodles and soup – meant we were skinny. My digestive system, which had not functioned properly for most of my life, was in full working mode. It was heavenly. I vowed to try to give up meat, or at least cut it right back; my body clearly did not need it, though already I knew I'd crave it from time to time. I especially loved red meat. I adore blue steaks, you know, where the meat is almost still wriggling. But since my body had started to function better, undigested food no longer pulled my energy down. Physical lightness was a refreshing experience; it was all the convincing I needed.

I'd proven I could cope well without luxuries. While sailing for the first nine years we didn't have a fridge or running hot water. Now, we had less, and not even a toilet! But toilets haven't been around since the beginning of time, and people survived. To me, it is a task of such small importance that as long as I can 'function,' then it is not a problem; I only needed a trowel and a thick bush!

Our muscles were strong; sinewy streaks lined our arms and thighs; our tummies were flat – it was a healthy way to live. But a painful one too!

Paul gave us some feed: we would replace it when we borrowed his car. The next camp was in the bush and not accessible via car, so we drove on to the following camp and were surprised to find the lady quite abrupt. The recommended camp at Providence was beside and part of a caravan park.

'No, you're not welcome – no one is on horses. The last lot we had here didn't clean up after themselves, so that's it.'

Noel's shoulders slumped, and I felt deflated like a withered balloon.

'Could we possibly store a bag of feed here, so if we camp down the road, we can collect it easily, for our boys?'

'No, it'd be in the garage and get eaten by rats; there's no point.'

With that we left. It was upsetting to be judged by others' thoughtlessness. Anyone who didn't want to help our boys instantly received an entry into my bad books. They didn't know how hard they worked!

We drove along to an alternative campsite and TSR at Denison. A large fenced paddock was available within the park. There were horses in the paddock and some outside. But we were not that worried; there were plenty of areas to fence off if necessary. At least we knew where we were heading.

We drove to the pretty town of Cooma and sourced a small lightweight gas camping stove to alleviate our load even further. We bought a twenty-kilogram bag of expensive feed and another bag of chaff: high calorie, full of goodness and vitamins. Back at the parkland, we found a small wooded area and, using rope, hauled the bags of food high into the trees, away from critters and, hopefully, prying eyes.

We spent five days at Paul's place in Yaouk. The boys had a good rest and ate plenty. We fully understood why most trekkers tackle the trail with a support vehicle; we were doing it the hard way. A car for the day made everything so easy. The horses' feed was heavy and cumbersome and a big burden to carry each day.

We'd cleaned our gear, washed our clothes, rested, repaired, and sewed. I could hang my underwear on the fence to dry instead of on the back of the saddle while we trekked. We helped catch horses and load gear and horses with Jane and Paul. Paul runs a trekking business; he has a good herd and obviously loves his horses. Jane was young, willing: she adored the horses too. They were a good team, and we were so grateful for Paul's generosity. We kept his number, should we need it. He understood our aches and pains. He told us we were doing well to be trekking for so long.

Our big row was way behind us now. My ankle still twinged from the beginning, but the argument of giving up was gone. I was glad, but I had reneged on the deal. We'd agreed that if one of us wanted to stop, then we were all going to stop. I had made Noel continue; I knew it was the right direction – for me.

We left Paul's and rode along a quiet roadway. Flat open plains at the start of the high country prompted positive thoughts. Our appreciation of the grandeur unfolding before us up-lifted our hearts; we finally felt that we were on the trail and not just following a national road system.

Biting My Feet

The trail improved, with wide soft footpaths dotted with the odd house where people would open gates for us, allowing us to skirt their properties. We climbed from 1,200 metres to 1,560 metres, and even the horses' eyebrows began sweating. We traversed around cattle grids and through gates without a drama. The packs stayed still, and the sun shone; a perfect day.

We approached a farmstead and walked along its borders to find two large dogs hanging by their back legs in a tree. They'd been shot. We could only assume they were wild dogs causing problems. Our boys ignored them. We traversed open reserves and meandered through creeks with trickling water so clear you hardly knew it was there.

On abundant grass we gave the boys time to have a pick. Charlie was too well fed and fit – he loved striding out so much he didn't want to eat! He started to fidget from foot to foot as if in need of a pee. He backed up; all Ned wanted to do was eat, but Charlie was a pain and prevented him from doing so. I tried to control Charlie, but as he reversed into the group, he lifted his leg half-up in the air and gently gave the nearest horse a shove! He doesn't kick; he just pushes, as if to say, *Come on, let's go!*

'Quit it, Charlie, stop being a pain,' I said. 'Just eat while you can.'

Charlie sighed and stood, sulking. Ned sliced the grass urgently with his teeth, his eyes watching Charlie, waiting for his next antics.

Charlie almost tapped his toes with impatience, then swung his big head back towards me and tried to nibble my foot. When he couldn't get a grip on my toes, he used his huge Roman nose to push at my leg, pestering. This boy made me laugh every day.

Eventually, we acquiesced to Charlie's demands, and I realised I had spoiled this boy rotten and he was the leader of *all* of us now, not just the other horses. I threw a quick, guilty glance at Noel, and he rolled his eyes.

Charlie raised his head high and pricked his ears; I could almost hear him whistle a happy tune. I peered down at the powerful muscles in his shoulders and neck, and a buzz of happiness whirled in my stomach. I couldn't help but smile. My scared boy was no longer a coward: he was a leader; he was strong, an explorer, loving life. It brought tears to my eyes.

I thought about them all. The surroundings were conducive to deep thoughts: the beauty of the hills, the open land, Australia. The people who had passed these horses on to us had missed out. All they needed was time, patience, and a bit of understanding. Understandably, though, not all relationships click. When Ned first arrived, he was petrified of everything. Now he knew he could conquer his fears and would do *anything* for us. On occasion, he would look at us to question, but once reassured, he had complete faith. He was one of the best little horses I had ever owned. He was pure joy; I could see his smile.

Stevie was still a bit aloof; previously he'd protest and put his ears back when Noel used leg aids, but he no longer did. For Noel rarely used leg aids; instead he talked to Stevie. They had a quiet bond; they took care of each other. Noel trusted him implicitly, and Stevie rewarded him back with his trust and affection. He may have still been aloof with me, but he adored Noel.

Spirit was the calm dude, so at ease to be packing: he preferred it to being ridden. Spirit allowed you to ride him but would protest here and there with a frustrating hesitation at a creek or a grumpy flick of the ears. But while packing he had fun. When we stopped, he'd sidle up to Noel and place his chin in Noel's lap and look up at him. Occasionally, he'd stick out his tongue and just hold it there, nudging Noel's leg to make sure he'd seen it. It made me laugh when he'd take Stevie's reins in his mouth and just hold them, as if to say, *I can do this, watch me.* Spirit had definite boundaries, and once he had us trained, we were all happy. He liked his own company; he, too, would wander off if not tethered!

Dom found life one big game. I'd not known a sweeter horse: he was always happy to see us and adored attention. He riled the others; when it was play time, he'd make them run. He wasn't suffering too badly being at the end of the pecking line.

Great chunks of sadness lingered in the pit of my stomach, knowing that they wouldn't always be with me. The pull to be with my family in the UK was still lurking, nibbling at the edges of my consciousness. But we had secured the horses' future. Racing cast-offs have an uncertain fate, which ranges from oblivion, to finding contented homes, and everything in between.

Our boys were loved, but not only that, they had something to give. They were not machines; they were purposeful and confident. They were brave, broken-in, handled, kind, and gave back so much more than anyone could possibly give them.

I knew I was too soft with them. They were disciplined but could push their luck without fear of too much of a telling off. I wondered if it was because relationships with animals are relatively short; there's no time to let love build slowly – it's instant. Subconsciously, when bringing a new animal into the folds of your family, you know that you will probably out-live it; it will pass away before you, and you'll have to deal with that. Is that why animal bonds can be so rapid, intensely deep, and incredibly emotional? Certainly, I have a passion for horses, but these boys made my heart swell. Perhaps it's all of those reasons and that they'd so dramatically changed from being a bit lost in the world, to having a purpose; a purpose they relished with unfettered success.

The woods yawned open, and we found Oldfields Hut. The hut was what I'd call a shed. But it had a lovely veranda, and it was private, quiet, welcoming. Two cyclists were already there, two chaps on a weekend ride, Nick and David.

'It's the weekend? I wouldn't have a clue.' Noel grinned.

They watched us unload the horses. 'Can we help?'

'Thanks, but no – we have an order of things now. Appreciate the offer, though.'

It'd probably take longer to explain what to do, and by now we weren't interested in thinking. We dumped the boys' gear and decided to walk them down to the creek for a drink. There was a small tank that was full of rain water that we'd utilise later, but for their first, long drink, we'd use the creek.

'It's not far.' Our cycling friends pointed down the hill.

It wasn't that far, but leading five horses that were on a permanent adventure, after a long ride, it felt like miles. We finally found the creek, and the boys dunked their noses in the cool stream and quenched their thirst.

Charlie had developed a new trick of shoving his head in the water up to his eyes, ensuring his nostrils were fully immersed, and then blowing bubbles. I had no idea what possessed him to do this, but he took much enjoyment from it. I could only relate to how Noel and I behave. Not that we blow bubbles in water – well, I know I don't. But since our relationship had been built on the back of mad-cap escapades, many times during our marriage we've put our lives in each other's hands. We'd built a bond between us that I'd only ever witnessed in movies. This bond and trust allowed us to be who we actually were. We never judged, embarrassed, or demoralised the other – there were no airs-and-graces: we were just us. I can't think of a greater gift to give someone. I can only assume that this is what Charlie felt. If he wanted to blow bubbles he could; he could chew my foot and dance. Charlie was being Charlie – what a freedom!

'Let's ride bareback on the way back; we don't need to walk,' said Noel, looking up towards the camp.

'We'll need to find something to step on – once upon a time I could just hop on, but that was over twenty years ago and on small ponies!' I replied.

We tried a few times to jump on Ned and Stevie, but they ended up throwing their ears back, and I didn't blame them. They had finished their day and didn't need us two hauling on their manes, whimpering and moaning, trying to climb up.

'You know what: without stirrups I can't get on! I used to just jump up and swing on, but I guess that was forty years ago. I think my strength-to-weight ratio may have been altered somewhat!' Noel grinned, his body bent, sucking in great gulps of oxygen.

Back at camp there was good grass, and we hitched the boys to the timber post and rail specifically made for this reason. They waited patiently; they knew the deal now. Noel and I pegged out their paddock and then let them wander off. They munched away happily. The kangaroos that grazed nearby didn't disturb them.

The cyclists were staying in the hut another night, despite a pesky possum making a racket up and down the chimney. We pitched our tents behind the shed, on a flat, protected spot. The cyclists watched us with interest.

'I can't believe you have so much to do and it takes so long!' they said, observing our ongoing labour.

'It takes the same time, if not longer, to pack up each day,' I explained. 'It is so much harder than we expected.'

'All we have to do is dismount and lean the bike up against a wall and that's it!' They laughed, we laughed too, but I'm not sure if it was in jest, or that little 'insanity' giggle, where you realise you are starting to lose it a bit.

On one end of the hut was a small empty room, and we put our equipment in there; it was a handy space.

The next morning we waved off the cyclists and enjoyed the solitude. We moved the paddock to fresh grass and let the boys do their thing.

We sorted through our gear, cleaned, repaired, brushed off sweat, and washed and aired everything we could. We dismantled our tents and put our beds in the hut. While we were enjoying a lunch, two walkers arrived, Simon and Di. They had trekked for two to three months and were on the last few days.

'Yes, just that part to tackle.' As they pointed up high into, what looked like cliffs, I breathed a sigh of relief; we had our boys to carry us, but we wouldn't be going up that high. Their gear was simple, the best, most expensive, light, and easy. We swapped details, as they were interested to hear how long we'd keep going – so were we!

They pitched their tents at the back of the hut while we enjoyed the luxury of a bench. But the tents would have been better. We spread our kitchen equipment on the small table in the hut, and Noel cleaned off the sticky, honey-like substance.

'Weird that those guys left it like that,' he commented.

That night the possum made himself known. *Scuttle, scurry, bang, crash, rummage* – the furry critter was making it clear that the hut was his home. We didn't sleep well. Noel chased him out two or three times during the night.

In the morning, the sticky, honey-like substance was back on the table.

'The bloody-thing peed all over the table!' We cleaned it again and decided to stay another night. There was plenty of water in the tank, enough to eat for the boys, and it was like having our own home, albeit a shed with a rude intruder.

The walkers left us with a cheery wave. We heard back from them some months later: they successfully completed their walk. Prior to departure, they had arranged food drops along the way. We realised that either a back-up car/van/person or food drops was a better way to do this trip. We were struggling and, to be honest, still not enjoying it that much, although I really wasn't ready to admit it.

The riding part was fun, but only part of it. Sore limbs, worrying over packs, and busy roads were the biggest part of the adventure. The secluded, grassy tracks were few and far between. When our limbs started to cry out in pain we couldn't wait to dismount.

On each dismount, I had to think carefully before I swung my leg over the back of the saddle. The ankle I had sprained in the beginning was not quite right: I still had to protect it. The ground was a long way down. My legs would be so stiff that they'd protest at suddenly having to bear my weight. My knees bent, not with elastic ease, but with crunching complaints.

After two full days' rest, we were ready to tackle the next part of the trip.

Fires Threaten

From Oldfields Hut the scrub track opened out into vast plains. The worry here was brumbies, not cars. Sighting only one stallion protecting his mare and foal, I was actually sad we hadn't seen more, although the horror stories of a wild herd trampling through a camp during the night, stealing your horses, were not too far from my thoughts. If threatened during the day, we planned to huddle together and make noise. We had originally carried whips to help protect ourselves, but these had long gone when weight became our first priority. We'd not practiced cracking the whips while mounted; I'm sure we would have created havoc.

This section led us through glorious countryside. The creeks we traversed were not a problem. The biggest challenge was preventing Dom rolling in the water. He'd give no warning, but if he hesitated, we had to yell at him straight away or he'd be down before we knew it.

The expanse of green that characterises Australia took my breath away. Unlike the rolling countryside of England, these plains were flat, yellow, tough – no-nonsense lands. Flexing its muscles, the Murrumbidgee River raced down to our feet, wide, strong, and active. So vastly alone, the horizon stretched out before us, inducing sensations of freedom, spirit, and hope. There was nothing to remotely hint at which decade we were in, just the hissing whisper of the breeze, creaking leather, and twenty hooves padding on the grass. I had been bedevilled by my emotions, guilt, worry, and responsibility. Momentarily they had faded away, allowing me to revel in nature's show and our combined achievements.

Ironically, although we'd achieved the craved-for sense of freedom, we'd also given it up. There's a compromise in most things and ours was a slice of that liberty – for how could we be free when the horses demanded so much of our attention, and needed constant care? It was a wonderful concession though, not one I resented in the slightest.

Three horses carried our worldly possessions; the other two were burdened with us. Not only were we modern day cowboys, we were bush cooks, farriers, vets, home-builders, counsellors (to each other and the horses). We became support, grooms, fence-constructors, navigators, seamstresses, leather-smiths, communication technicians, rope workers, and cleaners, while we trekked along bridle paths and springy turf.

It couldn't get much better than this, could it? I allowed myself to think. The boys' hooves beat in a neat line where the track narrowed, allowing single file only. I threw Ned's lead-rein over his neck, so as to avoid Charlie's tail. The narrow path broadened out once again to sloping hills and a small park where clean toilets with toilet roll were supplied, a convenient break for us. Sadly, a bit further on we met a long, wide tree trunk blocking our pathway. Smaller trees knitted together further on; we couldn't continue.

'We'll have to turn around,' I said. 'We're not going to get them past that tree, and the path looks so overgrown up ahead.'

Noel agreed.

Eventually, we reached beautiful plains where the white nude tree trunks had now been replaced with patches of green and pockets of blue. The old scrub gave way to new gums; vivid red-veins in new shoots twisted between dull green leaves to work in harmony. Tiny, intricate flowers poked through slithers of grass, blushes of pink, light mauves, and knee-high glowing yellows. A small herd of wild horses watched from a distance; the leader, a bold black stallion, pushed his herd in the opposite direction. Our boys wouldn't survive in the wild. Although they had toughened up, in comparison they were soft. We'd heard stories of a white stallion in this area that threatened walkers. We hoped to avoid him.

Along the by-way we met two enormous kangaroos that were quite content to sit right in the middle of the track. Charlie hesitated but didn't stop. As he walked towards them, his flicking ears told me he was wondering if he was doing the right thing; his tensing body gave me cause to grip a little harder with my knees. The roos stood their ground for a while until we were just a few metres away. I thought that either they were going to turn tail and run or we were. I hoped they would.

'Good boy, Charlie, good boy,' I said confidently, hoping he'd hang onto his self-assurance. His thumping heartbeat pounded on my leg. As we moved closer, the roos suddenly hopped off to our right and up the bank. All the boys were surprised, heads and ears up, but continued on. They had learned that they were one-up in the pecking order, and Charlie was loving being in charge, being the boss and the leader.

We had a soft tread beneath the hooves, padded by leaves and snapping twigs. Circuit Hut appeared from behind the thick grove of trees. There were four timber steps leading up to the front door, and a corrugated iron veranda extended across the front. Along the facade were four matching, russet-stained timber posts. Inside, the brown timber theme continued on the floor, walls, and ceiling. There was one double bedroom, two single bedrooms, and a kitchen/diner. The unused fridge (no power), candles, fireplace, and large sash windows were all welcomed. Newspaper had been left to help start a fire for the evening. The date was September 2013, just a few months old, so we read it first! Twigs and logs were stacked neatly by the fire. A frying pan, bush-saw, guest book, table, and two chairs were left for people like us, passers-by. We didn't use the bed-frames; our mattresses were too good. The frames were ideal for drying out sweaty blankets though, allowing us to brush them clean after they'd dried.

We noticed how strong our knees had become with crouching down so often. Never had our bottoms and hips been so delighted and quite relieved that we had chairs to sit in.

These huts are a marvellous idea. You must leave the hut how you found it, for the next travellers. They are located too far to be ruined by vandals, but situated within forests begging to be explored.

The lush grazing amid the trees helped us all settle in quickly. Water was a struggle with the creek barely a trickle. On arrival into camp, the boys would drink a couple of buckets of water each, their thick tongues hanging loose, dripping cool water to wherever their heads swung. After a short break they'd drink the same again. Regularly climbing a steep bank with two ten-litre buckets of water was helping our muscles to build.

It was here, at Circuit Hut, I found a small square mirror in my compass case. Protected in the case, it had survived, but I had forgotten I had it. Without thought of the horrors I may find, I flicked open the lid, and a stranger peered back at me. Thick grey strands had taken root in my fringe, hinting at a *Cruella de Vil* look. I had wide, white horizontal lines between my eyes and above my nose where I'd creased my face in worry and the sun hadn't reached inside the folds. With my dirty t-shirt, cracked lips, and damaged skin and hair, I looked quite a picture. I looked down at my short nails: they were dirty and chipped. My fingers were smudged with 'Neddy-dirt' where I'd recently scratched his tail. 'In for a penny, in for a pound,' I muttered as I hiked up my trouser leg. My neglected, milk-white legs were stark, almost blindingly white, the hairs making an impressive take-over bid that would match any man's!

I sighed and grinned. I may have been a mess, but I was a happy mess. I glanced at Noel. His thick beard was a tangled bird's nest, flecked with strong greys, each flamboyant strand with a mind of its own. His hair needed a cut, and the sun had etched itself onto his skin. Overall, 'haggard' would be the picture caption beneath us both. The boys didn't worry what we looked like as long as they were fed, so I wouldn't worry.

The weather was hotting-up, and this was not the place to be in summer. Bush fires were becoming a concern. Fires were a relatively new event for me to think about, as I had grown up in the UK. I could tell Noel was uncomfortable with where we were, which worried me. He regularly listened to the weather reports on the radio, and lately he'd become twitchy and unsettled if he'd not heard an update for a few hours. We'd been warned that if we were caught, we should just let the horses go; they'd figure it out – 'you'll die trying to save them.' Even with this sobering thought, I was quite sure I'd put my life at risk to help them.

If you've not witnessed a fire, even on the news, let me explain. Gum trees contain eucalyptus oil, which is highly flammable. The oil explodes – the trees literally blow up. Fire moves fast in a strong wind, faster than you can run. The direction can shift. It is lethal, terrifying, deadly.

In January 2003, bushfires sparked by lightning strikes burned for weeks, four people died, four hundred and ninety were injured, and over five hundred houses were destroyed. Seventy percent (164,000 hectares) of ACT burned. In addition, fire raged through the alpine areas of the Snowy Mountains, threatening the town of Jindabyne, terrifying the residents. Much of the area we were in and around was either burned already or currently threatened by fire.

In the spring of 2013, when we set off, it was the warmest NSW September on record. There were a series of bushfires in September and October; they peaked on the 18th of October with one-hundred fires burning across NSW state – as of the 19th of October, two hundred and forty-eight houses had been destroyed.

With our small portable radios we listened religiously to the weather forecast. We had an agreement: with the slightest threat, we'd retreat to safety immediately.

It was Monday; the forecast for Friday was thirty-six degrees and rising each day. During our last meeting with Anne, we had guessed when we would see her next, but we needed to let her know exactly when and where.

We could afford a couple of days' rest here: the boys had a good fill, and we had two good nights' sleep. The day before leaving we packed everything we possibly could.

'It's a full moon; why don't we get up at three and try and get moving by six?' Noel suggested. 'Then we may miss the heat of the day.'

That sounded good to me. It would be dark, but we'd have the moonlight. We didn't have to pack our tents, just bedding. We made some sandwiches and left out the billy and all the tea-making equipment.

Bad Timing

As the moon hung high, we rose and slurped hungrily at our tea, itching to organise the packs. The boys were a bit surprised to be caught in the dark. They stood patiently while we saddled them up. The fence was the hardest to take down. Up and down banks, across a creek. The way we worked together, busy, non-stop, should have meant packing up was quick. It wasn't: it always took more than three hours, no matter what we did. This time we had started at 3 a.m. and were ready to leave by 5.30 a.m., a record for us.

As dawn tickled the sky, and shafts of light broke through the trees, we were ready to go. I wore a cotton t-shirt with a light cotton shirt over the top to protect my skin from the sun that I knew would beat down on us later.

My knees poked through my jeans, the hems swept the floor, and the crotch sagged. The once upon a time tight t-shirts hung limp on our sinewy bodies. We punched new belt holes into the cracking leather regularly.

More often our worries were immediate, with no time or desire to think of tomorrow or next week, only the now: chafing, sores, feed, the right decisions, rest, safety – all thoughts in the moment, here and now. The thinking process changed with summer slowly gathering momentum: potential bush fires threatened; we had to ensure we were safe.

Muted by the mist, the early morning colours set the composition; the sun started to burn off the fog, revealing snippets of blue sky above the sweet-smelling gully of old forest, our stomping ground. The striking sun lit the remaining languid swirls of white cloud and made a garden of eerie fantasy where one would expect elves or fairies to appear. Nature's stillness held promise of a wonderful day. The thick scrub crowded at our sides, hiding the shy kangaroos, but we all knew they were there.

We made our way through the timber throng. Charlie didn't like the mist: he could hear movement but not see what was making it. Instead of striding forward and being the leader, he became hesitant, unsure. I couldn't blame him: it did feel like we were on the set of a horror movie. The last of the swirling fog hid snapping twigs and furtive movements.

'Are you happy to go in front for a while, until Charlie settles?'

'Sure,' said Noel, and I stopped my group while his three marched off in front. Stevie wasn't worried and was glad to be in front. Charlie and Ned scurried up behind the other three so tight that their heads butted tails – we moved as one. Ned cast furtive glances behind, just to make sure the monsters weren't closing in.

As the heat slowly crept across the land, the flies came. It was hard to converse and avoid swallowing one. They gathered at the corners of our eyes, and so many sat on our backs that we thought of employing crowd control. They bothered the horses too – we put nets on them and on us – but then we all sweated. At times the sweat was better than the flies for me. Mostly, we kept the nets off the boys when they worked. During their rest time, if the flies still persisted, then we'd put the nets on them. It must've been a relief from the incessant flies on their eyes. It's a satisfying noise, that whomp, when you've just splatted a fly.

The mist started to thin; the sun was throwing its rays down with vigour. The bush continued its horror-movie theme. Dead, bleached trees accompanied us for several kilometres. Only the most tenacious growth poked through but had soon withered and died, a bush graveyard.

As we pushed along the eerie by-way, the scenery slowly changed. Bright growth waved as we breezed past, and soon we were approaching Wadens Gap. A pretty creek babbled through the terrain, and sprays of greens seemed to fight for supremacy, emitting a lush smell of new life.

We had already driven to the next camp in Paul's car. We'd tied the feed in the trees. I hoped it was safe and that thoughtless kids hadn't hacked it down for a brief bit of fun.

During the day we tried to follow the advised route of the electric pylons. The route was straight, clear, wide, and free of traffic; however, the pylons were pitched along the shortest distance, which meant we climbed up and down vast hills. Neither horses nor riders enjoyed this. It lengthened the journey and made us all tired and cranky. To our right we could see the road following the contours. After bemoaning the amount of roadwork we had to do, suddenly we were glad to be able to find one!

At the bottom of a dip we found a way out and gladly stepped onto a fairly wide country road. It was quiet, and there was a scratch of verge. We breathed a collective sigh of relief. The boys strode out and I am sure were grateful for the easier ride.

After a few kilometres, we were on a track once again; it was windy but flat, quiet, soft. The heat was becoming heavy, drawing our energy away.

'Thank goodness we knew not to stop at Providence,' Noel said.

'It worked out well – we do have to do some extra kilometres, but at least we know where we're going.'

We both found that our bodies 'wound-down' with an approaching campsite – so if we hadn't been aware that we could not stop at the first one, those extra miles would have stretched into slow agony.

The track wove down until we could see the main road we had to cross. The small parking area gave us a moment to dismount, stretch our legs, and have a pee behind the twiggy bushes. The boys stood calmly and waited for us to do what we had to do. It probably involved a Snickers bar. The boys had learned not to ask for our food; they had grass, and we let them eat when we could.

Noel and I were watching the road. I am not sure what Noel was thinking, but I was worrying about large trucks. Ned was better but still didn't like them. I'd noticed that with age, I worried more. I hated it; this wasn't me. I was a strong woman in mind and body. I had to give myself a good slap around the chops (metaphorically) to snap out of it. It was an easy road to slip down. I'd witnessed it happen to a woman I knew – actually two. Getting older means you think more about physical pain; you know how much it is going to hurt when you fall off or something goes wrong. It can prevent you taking steps into a new escapade, getting out there, being adventurous. Fortunately, I have a group of woman friends who are incredibly strong. They look at me sideways if I hesitate at doing something. Being surrounded by tough women has made me stronger. I will not slip into a scared, withered person, by mind or by physical strength.

I enjoy a challenge and extracting myself from that protective cocoon of normalcy. But I revelled in it when it was hard. When I didn't have time to eat, when I put others first, when it was a struggle. That made it all the sweeter, the winning. I had not failed at one challenge yet, and I knew I'd regret it deeply if I failed now. I straightened my shoulders and looked around at our motley crew. But they were no longer motley: gleaming coats, bright eyes, and a questioning look towards me.

Are we going now?

Where are we going?

Do you have plenty of feed?

This family was all I needed, and I gave a contented sigh, which was mixed with that delicious exhaustion that comes with working hard to get to where you want to be.

Suddenly, though, my heart rate jumped, and I flew into crises mode.

'Quick, QUICK, get Spirit; he's going down!' Spirit had folded up his front legs and was on his way to going right down. I don't know if he intended to roll or rest.

'Up, UP,' I yelled from the front of the pack, Charlie and Ned raising their heads to see what I was screeching at.

Noel ran over to Spirit and made him change direction and stand up.

'Your horse is so pesky.' I grinned.

'Was he rolling or resting?' Noel voiced my thoughts.

'I don't know; he was probably going to roll, letting us know it is time to get moving – he's had enough of carrying our gear. Either that or something is up and he's having an off day. I hope nothing is rubbing.'

Noel rolled his eyes, with no attempt at secrecy; I always turned everything into a worry. I didn't worry about me, or Noel, just the boys. Noel checked over his pack, more to alleviate my concerns than anything else, and all was well.

We mounted up and discussed crossing the road. We had only two kilometres to traverse.

'Okay, you go in front once we have crossed; then if Ned takes off he has something to run into,' I said.

'He'll be fine; you'll be fine.' Noel smiled.

'Yeah, you're right – now we'll cross together: get ready to push them forward sharply.'

Noel knew the drill, so did the boys. That's the one thing about Noel and me: we can remind each other of the obvious. He didn't need telling, neither did I. But we both repeated to each other the safety aspect and the best way to handle whatever we were tackling.

'Once committed, keep going,' said Noel, while checking left then right.

'Right, ready?'

'Let's go – it's clear.'

'Goooo-onnn – T-rotttt.'

We both called our signal to our boys, and they duly responded. Immediately, we were safely on the other side, and we assumed our agreed positions with Noel in front. When the road narrowed, we squeezed our legs together and pushed the boys quickly along the slender stretch.

Soon the short track appeared, with the paddock gate at the end, and we gratefully turned away from the road. The gate was slightly open, the string undone.

'If this is our paddock, we'll have to check this gate each day: someone's left it open.' This 'paddock' was huge, about fifty acres, undulating with thick bunches of trees, scrub, and ditches. On our prior visit, horses had been grazing in here. We weren't sure if they were wild or not, as some had been inside the paddock and some out.

Once inside, we closed the gate and secured it with the ratty string. We spent a few minutes studying our bearings and headed to the clearing at the end of the field. There were no horses in sight.

It was around 3 p.m., and we were all relieved when we found our camp spot. Just inside the fence there was a clutch of trees, flat grass, timber to sit on, and a bit of shelter and privacy from the track. The trees were perfect for tying up the boys. We could drop our gear right where we'd camp.

I was concerned with the fencing: we needed to ensure that they couldn't get out on the road or tangle in loose wire. Before resting, drinking, or eating, we found the creek.

'We ought to walk around the fence perimeter and ensure it's all okay,' I said.

'Okay, let's go.'

We walked the entire perimeter, checking the fence, making repairs, and throwing out pieces of broken wire. Two hours later, tired and thirsty, we were lost! We must've been the first people ever to get lost in a paddock!

My head felt light, dizzy. I was finding it hard to walk, and I realised I'd eaten only four biscuits during the day. We eventually found our camp, and we both sat and ate some salami on crackers. I tried to drink as much as I could; I knew I had a 'head' coming.

Slowly our camp took shape. I was drinking and drinking, trying to fight off the problems I knew I'd have with a migraine. It was my own stupid fault. I was dehydrated and hungry. I was middle-aged, no longer twenty when I could go all day without eating and drinking. I had to ensure I rehydrated regularly, or pay the price. I was going to suffer, but it couldn't have been at a worse time.

I sat quietly and watched as other trekkers returned to the TSR. They told us they rented these paddocks. I was starting to struggle but didn't want to show I was having problems. There wasn't much grass in the TSR; there was more in the park. So Noel and I pegged out a corral, and the boys gladly let us lead them to more food.

'Our boss has just phoned,' one of the trek leaders said. 'You're invited to dinner.'

'That's great!' Noel enthused while I smiled through the pain that had hold of my head.

'Bring your laundry too, all of it, and shower gear.'

'Thank you, that's nice of you.' I smiled a practised smile, trying to show some enthusiasm for something that would've been wonderful at any other time. We had an hour or so to arrange our campsite and gear, so I swallowed more pills, more water, and shut my eyes and prayed that I could beat this one.

Why now? I muttered.

We sat with a small group of trek leaders and riders; gentle conversations were easy. The car came to collect us, and within fifteen minutes we were at a country house surrounded by meadows with the splendid scent of roast lamb tickling the taste buds.

This was the last night of trekking for a large group that had spent a week or two together. There was a chef working magic in the kitchen, bottles of superb wine for all to enjoy, soft sofas, kindred spirits, fun conversations, and comfort.

After two loads of washing, Noel and I were shown to a bathroom each. While our washing dried we spent several greedy minutes under steaming water, armed with scrubbing brushes, soap, and shampoo. Soft towels on heated rails caused low groans of appreciation.

I tried the 'ignore it and it will disappear' theory through the first course of salad. I started partaking in an interesting conversation with a father and daughter who had been trekking together as part of the group. I assembled a green forkful, hoping my stomach would hold onto it.

'Main course is ready; please line up here,' someone called, and it was then I knew I'd lost the battle.

The pink folds of steaming lamb were professionally cut from the leg as we approached with warm plates in our wind-worn hands. I swallowed the saliva, but not because of the lamb. The other guests were making appreciative noises.

'Hey, Noel,' I whispered, 'erm, take this – I need some air.' Noel's mouth bowed down as he took my plate, his eye-brows jerked together.

'You okay?'

'Yes, I'll be fine. Don't worry about me, just enjoy; take your time.' I forced the corners of my lips up, and before anymore could be said, I turned and strode to the back door. As the weathered door swung back behind me, the swelling talk and laughter inside muted. With utter relief I found peace, quiet, and shade.

'Are you okay?' My empty chair had been noticed.

'Yes, fine,' I called back as brightly as I could. 'I just have a bit of a headache, which makes me feel a bit off. Just bad luck, bad timing, please go enjoy yourselves – tell Noel I am fine and take your time.' I sat on a stone wall with green moss peeling from the top, my eyes cast down to help ease the throbbing beat behind them, a clear indication I did not want to talk either.

After an hour or so, the pain owned my head. Self-pity swirled in my stomach alongside hunger pangs, but I couldn't eat. In the company of misery, I cursed my own body for its inconsiderate timing.

'How you doing?' Noel finally appeared. I could almost feel his contented stomach.

'I'd like to go home.' As I spoke, the owner stepped out behind Noel, and I made my apologies.

'Don't worry, I understand; it's just a shame you missed it all.' She handed me a large plate of food, covered in aluminium foil. 'Here's a plate for tomorrow – you can have yours then,' she said, slipping her free hands into jean pockets.

'Thanks so much,' I said, and I meant it. I clutched the plate, and it shook a little. I knew I'd be ravenous by morning.

Driving home, Noel and a stable girl brushed over life and all its idiosyncrasies in fifteen minutes, as only you can do with strangers. Indicating goodbye and thanks with the flap of my hand, I vaulted over the disorder in our campsite, swallowed two pain-killers, and slumped into my tent fully-clothed. I gratefully slid into a deep sleep within my little dome of blue canvas heaven.

Noel checked the horses, topped up their water, and tidied the camp. The following morning Noel and I tucked into my dinner. It was fabulous and just what I needed.

The Beginning of The End

Anne was due a visit; we just had to ring her. We knew there was a phone a few kilometres north at Providence.

Our mobile phone was hardly used; we rarely had a signal. I have a love-hate relationship with phones and the internet. While sailing we didn't succumb to the technology; we enjoyed the complete package of freedom on the ocean. I find it a relief when I'm not expected to be contactable or to make contact regularly – it takes life to another level; you can really disappear. I remember when I passed my driving test when I was seventeen. The first time I drove alone, I was ridiculously excited to be able to go wherever I chose. No one knew where I was; I could turn left here, or right there, and only I made that decision.

I rode Dom, as he hadn't been ridden in many weeks; Noel fancied riding Spirit. All the horses called to each other as we separated them. Dom answered the urge to call back with a long scream, each time. He was hesitant and babyish, quite hard work for a simple hack. Spirit did all of what was asked and gave Noel a pleasant hour's ride to Providence and the pay phone.

We left a message for Anne, and Noel rang his brother Colin. The longing for home, familiarity, and family tugged at us both – a unique emotion, for we're usually quite content with our nomadic lifestyle.

We trekked home, the horses striding out, realising they were heading back to their mates. Up hills, small paths, grass-carpeted tracks, stepping around memories and previous footfalls. The vast vistas of green and blue were stunning and a balm for our weary bodies.

The fresh air tantalised other senses; so sweet was the perfume carried along by the breeze it induced memories of my happy childhood, and summertime in England.

We unsaddled outside the electric fence, and I held Dom and Spirit while Noel switched the battery power off. By now the wind was picking up, so we were glad to let the boys go. I unfastened the fence from one of the poles and lay two other poles down flat, so it would be safe to step over. I handed Spirit back to Noel and put my foot on the fence, so it was completely flat on the grass for Dom. Spirit walked over first. As Dom was half-way across, a gust of wind picked up the electric fence and a plastic pole, causing the fence to raise higher, and it tickled the front of Dom's back legs.

The boys were all crowded together, and Dom panicked. I was right in the middle of the herd.

In my mind, I had a fleeting vision of Dom galloping off with the electric fence around his back legs, with me dragging behind in a tangle of wire, Dom becoming further entangled, panicking, and breaking a leg. Then, in what felt like slow motion, my head turned in time to see the white strand hurtle towards my legs as Dom took flight, dragging it with him, not in my imagination this time, but in reality. And there was nothing I could do.

The horses didn't flatten me, but my legs where whipped out from under me. It was as if the solid ground had risen up and slapped my body with all its might. Dom was careening off, flat out with all his buddies. I fell hard onto my right thigh.

If there was a 'right' side to fall on, that was it, I thought cheerily. For this was bruise-free, so far. *Not anymore,* I thought.

Then the pain set in. Something irreversible had happened to my ankle; I was on the floor gasping in pain, and my ankle was seized in agony. *Had I broken it?* I sobbed; something twanged in my body, but I didn't know what: everything hurt and pulsed. Noel ignored the horses. Dom was no longer tangled, and they were eating as if nothing had happened.

Noel carried me to shade. I couldn't stand. I felt pathetic, tired, old. The fence was still down. Noel shooed the horses back into the corral and stood the fence back up. I sat still, stunned, snivelling, wiping my running nose on my arm. As Ned broke out, I tried to stand to help, but with a yelp I plumped back down. With a slow appraisal, I realised I was not too bad: shaken up, bruised, but nothing broken. My other ankle was twice as painful as the first twist; limping on two feet was going to make life interesting. I was teary all day. Eventually I could move, but not without great pain.

Swatches of deep bruising throbbed below the skin on my right thigh – the only thigh I had been able to sleep on. My last fall from Charlie had bruised my left thigh severely; the purples had not yet turned yellow – the pain was still raw. Now I had more bruising on the other thigh. I couldn't sleep on my back or my front. I had run out of options.

That night in the tent I had to rig my body in a half-forward, half-side position. My hips were too painful to lean on. My boobs morphed from small mounds to enormous globes if I tried to lie on my front. I rolled clothes up in front and behind me, so I could lay diagonally forward or back – I still slept soundly!

The stiffness didn't last too long, and we sourced richer grass with a flowing creek at the bottom of a hill. We tied up the boys, took down the fencing, then led them and carried the fence half a kilometre down the hill. Ned was following. Noel and I led two each. Ned trotted up behind Stevie and nipped his bottom. Stevie ran straight into Noel, and this tipped his emotions over the edge. He'd watched the fence flatten me, and now he was almost flattened too.

'Hey!' he yelled. 'These horses are going to kill us! Oceans are much safer!' He then proceeded to engage in a long and vivid swearing fit. The rest of us were wrapped in a cloak of austere astonishment.

Noel's lungs finally expired of air, and as the silence claimed back the day, we all sedately walked on.

'I can't believe I can yell like that,' he said sheepishly.

I grinned. I'm not sure if I thought it was funny or was teetering on the cliff of insanity.

Later we checked the horses and sat on the side of the hill. The boys were safe; no harm had been done. We watched the pink and yellow sun set along the horizon. It was moments like these that made it all worth it: the easy warmth of the end of a day, the evening song of birds, the buzz of insects, and a plane humming overhead. The light faded from blue to dove-grey. We sat together and sighed, wrapped up in the romance of the moment. Noel's eyes crinkled at the corners, and he looked deeply into mine. He smiled dreamily, and I knew my man's romantic side was about to steal the show. As he drew in a breath, he suddenly stopped, clutched his neck, and choked on the enormous fly he'd just swallowed. He spent the next ten minutes spluttering. The moment was somewhat lost!

The trekking company came back the following day to transport their horses to another paddock. They brought us a care package of yoghurt, chocolate, biscuits, avocado, and two beers, all gratefully received.

I was still sore and tearful and close to giving up. The trekking was a big effort when you felt well, so it became an awkward struggle when engulfed in pain. I felt culpable all over again, as Noel wasn't telling me his true feelings – or not bothering to say he wanted to stop any longer – as he had a few weeks ago when he said he wanted to stop. I'd twisted myself into such a state; he daren't mention it again!

It was Noel's birthday.

'I hope you don't expect much,' I said. 'Well, actually, expect nothing!'

'Just one day without almost dying would be lovely.'

This was Noel's birthday wish. An ungainly guffaw burst from my lips. My laughter turned into a delirious cackle; plump tears plopped into my lap. I was no longer sure if I was laughing or crying. But I also felt guilty. I'd made him continue on a trip when he didn't want to. I had some thinking to do: my doubts were spreading and becoming more expressive than my convictions.

Lying in bed, ankles smarting, bruised, battered, and another headache beginning (which I daren't tell Noel about as I sounded so pathetic), thoughts of giving up tantalised my emotions. I tried to straighten my bed sheet, pushing it into the sleeping bag. Each movement was carefully choreographed. I had to think about which way to turn before I moved. Not only were my ankles stinging and my bruising throbbing, but if I bent my knees I suffered with wild cramp. The only way to deal with the cramp was to stretch my leg out straight and pull my toes back to counteract it. When I lifted my leg, and therefore my ankle, I wanted to scream. I clutched at my toes and started crying with the effort and pain! I ended up in a rather odd position a bit like a pointer dog, except I was pointing with my left leg. Hot tears and watery snot were running down my face. I couldn't wipe my nose as my hands were holding me up! Another undignified snort escaped from my lips (as if I could be any more undignified than I already was). I tittered manically, my laughter fled out of control, and a little sob broke free from my lips. The ridiculous position was making my stomach cramp with laughter.

I'd win at playing Twister though.

I stuffed a blanket in my mouth to prevent myself from yelling out – all this in a one-man tent! I was a little relieved no one could see me.

The moment passed, and I calmed down and popped another pill; two weren't enough. I wormed my way into bed, careful not to slide on my chafed bottom. I read four lines of my book before drifting into a deep sleep.

That night we were awoken by what sounded like a fire cracker. It wasn't too close, so we didn't worry. In the morning we found possum pee all over our tents. The cheeky critter stayed up in the tree above us and systematically peed down syrup-like liquid – another little delight when living in the bush! It hadn't rummaged in our food store though. The two tents faced each other with a tarp over both: the bags were in the middle, with the food carefully packed away, the scents trapped between our camping gear. Perhaps his night-time antics were in protest to being unable to reach a snack.

It was the day Anne was visiting. We'd provided instructions to our location, but we were hidden, off the track. We dug out a black marker pen and wrote 'Anne' on a yellow bucket with an arrow pointing towards us and placed it on the edge of the dirt track.

Fat streams of salty tears ran down my grubby face when Anne arrived. My entire body hurt, and I was pathetically sorry for myself. Her warm hug calmed me down.

She arrived armed with a symphony of delicious food: moist cake, fresh fruit and crisp vegetables, some chocolate, and a chicken dinner that was already prepared – we were half dazed by the abundance. We caught up on events, and the conversation turned to taking a break.

'We may see if we can rent a property with grazing for a few weeks,' Noel explained.

'The threat of fire is close too,' I added. 'We need to be somewhere safe.'

Anne gave us her full support and a shoulder to lean on. What a sight for sore eyes (and bodies) she was.

We drove to the small village of Adaminaby. In the cosy cafe I refrained from ordering the entire left side of the menu and settled for a hamburger, which I more or less inhaled. Meanwhile, Anne ate delicately, making us feel like Neanderthals, which I guess we were by this stage. Our spirits lifted. I searched for light trousers to replace my cotton trousers that had almost fallen apart, but everything was either too big or too small.

Fashion has never been important to me. In my early twenties I did wear fashionable clothes only because all my friends did, and it was expected of me in the work place. I've never been a 'shopper,' and I've never owned a credit card. Through our travels of sailing and trekking, clothes, jewellery, and makeup have become 'things,' such very unimportant 'stuff.' I do like to dress smartly on occasions; I like clean clothes, but fashion? I'd rather spend my money on life.

We shopped for the next trip; we were doing all the right things to continue.

I caught up with family and friends on the internet, while Noel and Anne took a quick sprint back to Yaouk (Paul's place) to collect a few items we had left behind.

We asked several people if there were places to rent in the area. 'Rarer than hens' teeth,' was the demoralising response. We couldn't stop here.

Too soon we were back and at camp, and the boys benefited from Anne's visit too, gratefully munching the sweet carrots. We all agreed that we'd stay in a hotel at Khancoban, the next village, and have a big celebration when we reached there. It would be a round, six-hour driving trip for Anne and a good few days trekking for us.

All too soon, Anne had to leave. Noel and I served the horses their evening meal and realised that we had forgotten to purchase batteries for the waning torches!

The following day we hitch-hiked back into Adaminaby. The next part of the trail was remote with few opportunities to shop: we needed good batteries; they were the only light we had. I took the opportunity to purchase more toilet rolls, muttering, 'You can never have too much.' I slid some extra packets of oats into my basket too.

'We need more oats,' I said.

'I know you are buying it for the horses!' Noel laughed. 'I don't know why I bother!'

Before making use of the internet in the shop I paid for our goods. As I held out my hand for the change, I noticed the 'Neddy-dirt' on the ends of my fingers, black smudges like burnt skin. My short nails were stubby; they somehow clung to the dirt beneath them and no amount of prodding would make it budge. I felt scruffy but powerful. I was fit, I knew my mind; I was in pain, and strong, and weak all at once. The tumultuous sensations didn't worry me any more – my mind was in constant disarray. The shop keeper sold me vitamin tablets that would help with the cramps; they were four years out of date – I ate them.

Outside the small supermarket and next to a large bin, with great satisfaction I diligently removed all excess packaging from our shopping. Then we nipped back into the supermarket for the internet, chatting with Sue via Facebook. We hoped that she would want to ride with us.

Why don't you come and join us for a bit? we wrote. *We'll give you one of the quietest boys to ride, come and see how you go.*

This offer was for Sue, to help build her confidence – she'd had a nasty fall some time ago – but it was for us too. We would have liked some company, and we were desperate for support.

Sadly, it didn't fit in with timing with other events in Sue's and Bill's busy lives.

We were grateful for shade at camp Denison, so we sat out the hot weather. 'Tomorrow it cools down a bit,' Noel said after listening to the forecast. 'Shall we make a move?'

'Okay,' I agreed, trying to ignore the pain and swelling in my ankle.

The flies were incessant; when one flew into my tea it was quite normal to flick it out and carry on drinking. I'd lost count of the flies we'd swallowed. I guess it was good protein, but one doesn't like to think too hard about where the flies were beforehand.

We sorted our clothes and took a shower.

'You've got a waist!' Noel said to me.

In my forties middle-aged-spread gleefully took over, but my waist was making a come-back. I guess starvation does that to you.

I slipped on a clean t-shirt with a grin, and within minutes that was filthy. My worn jeans and un-brushed, tangled hair clutched into a band were part of everyday life.

That afternoon we looked through the maps, studying the track to Khancoban. The stirring of excitement wafted in the air, but it was still a struggle for Noel.

'Are we carrying on then?' Noel asked. He looked at me with a glimmer of hope in his eyes and sighed. 'You want to go on, don't you?'

It was my turn to heave a sigh: I hurt all over, the fires were coming, and Noel wanted to stop, but I still had the desire to continue. I felt scared of *not* continuing – what would I have to face if we stopped? Was it *enough* to experience what we had?

'Well, we'll see,' I said, trying to accept the inevitable.

In the evening, we moved the boys from the paddock that was out of sight; we were packing in the morning, so we wanted them nearby. We put them in the smaller paddock within the TSR, but they just stood there looking at us – there was no feed. So I decided to make another corral just outside the main fence, where there was some green pick.

'They'll be okay for the night,' Noel said, sitting down, trying to enjoy a cup of tea.

'It's not enough for them; they'll be working all day tomorrow!' I said, exasperated. The boys had put on weight, and I wanted to keep it on. Noel was tired and wanted us to look after ourselves a bit, and he was right. I was working myself into a frazzle.

'I'll do it myself,' I said unreasonably.

I limped around and led them into the new paddock, feeling better. It was getting dark, but we just managed to slip their boots on before we could no longer see. It was going to be another early start.

At 4.45 a.m. we were almost ready, but the misty rain was irritating; we were all a bit out of sorts. As we finished the last strapping-on, I tripped over a bag handle, my recently injured ankle taking the full brunt, and I fell to the floor crying. We both stopped and tried to get a handle on our situation.

The feeling of something curiously fragile floated in the air, and my tight tummy flip-flopped with imprecise emotions – I couldn't put my finger on it. The horses were troubled, my teeth were clenched, and an uncomfortable silence hung over us. It was not a premonition, but a fear maybe? I'm not sure if my heavy limbs, weighted by fatigue, were warping my thoughts. Or the exhaustion of carrying guilt and responsibility too high, all the time, was sending me a message. It was useless trying to catalogue my emotions: it seemed I could no longer control them at all.

227

We were both feeling angst at the time and effort it took to get ready, bruises twanging, pains nagging; we were both short-tempered and tired even though we'd had a reasonable rest. It shouldn't be like this: these should be happy times.

Before my fears grew to mythical proportions, we silently finished packing; Noel watched me limping.

'How are you going to do a whole day on horseback in the state you're in?'

We both paused with a moment's introspection.

The day was grey, the horses weren't happy, we weren't happy.

'If we don't go,' I said, 'I might ring up for a truck.' I'd ignored my body's haggard entreaties for too long.

'It feels a bit like that, doesn't it?' Noel said. His words became a sad note hanging in the air between us.

We continued to pack and decided to walk around the corner to see what happened. I managed to haul myself up onto Charlie, but I'm not sure how. When I rotated my foot into the stirrup, the pain brought tears to my eyes. My ankle could bear little weight, so movement and weight together was agony. I felt that this was the beginning of the end.

We were underway and followed the river for twenty minutes until we came across a wonderful camp. Lush grass, startling vistas, water nearby, open paddocks for the boys, and flat camping for us. Even though it took twelve times longer to pack up than it did to get there, we stopped, unpacked, and made camp.

Was I really going to give this all up? My thoughts gathered momentum again to torture my plans. I had wanted adventure, but when we had talked about 'what next' I didn't want to sail again – not yet. I loved the independence of sailing, but I couldn't stand the thought of doing more exhausting night-watches, I didn't want to battle storms, sea-sickness, and such vulnerability. But now I had learned that you can have that vulnerability on land too – we were often moments away from serious situations. Our mortality is as delicate as lace, whether on tempestuous oceans within the hands of Mother Nature or astride once-wild beasts that carried the load of their own demons and ghosts.

I was becoming more aware of my mortality; I guess that happens with getting older. I thought the oceans would be so final if there was an accident, but on horseback in the bush, it was the same.

I looked up into the distant hills that would have been our next pathway. I couldn't only consider my needs and desires, my fears and anxieties; Noel had wanted to stop for some time. Perhaps it was lucky I had had my falls and injuries. Maybe in the bush, farther away from help, we would have run into more trouble. But most of all I would have forced Noel to continue. That wasn't our agreement, and more importantly, it wasn't the basis of a healthy relationship.

My self-counselling session came to an abrupt end when the mobile phone sprung into life alerting us of messages. Sue and Bill were passing through and looking for us. Sue, too, had been wonderful support.

As I tried to dial her number, we spotted a truck in the distance, rumbling our way. With big grins, Sue and Bill stepped out. It was lovely to see them.

With heartfelt hugs, we caught up on events. We shared a sip of wine each, and they cooked us dinner in their camping van. It was so luxurious to sit on cushioned seats. We talked about giving up, resting, stopping.

'You've done amazingly well – do whatever you need to do,' they said.

We are so lucky to have such great friends.

The rain pitter-pattered all night. The following day we decided to ring Paul from Yaouk to see if he was free to take us back to Kangaroo Valley.

Here's My Heart

Christmas Eve, after a nine hour truck ride, we were back in Kangaroo Valley. We paid Paul and thanked him. The boys were surprised to be back home. I wondered if they had a pang of regret.

'My goodness, they look well!' Clive said as I handed him two boys while we unloaded the rest. 'Just let them go here and come and have a cuppa.'

We released the boys, and they gratefully munched on the best paddock on the property. Andrea hauled our gear into her car and ferried it over to the spare cottage, before we'd gathered our wits. The welcome was unsurpassed, but wouldn't end there.

We sat and talked to Andrea and Clive; they put on hold umpteen jobs while listening to our story. We gratefully picked up the invisible threads of familiarity. When the light started to mute, I searched for the horses – they weren't in sight.

'Come on, jump on the golf cart: we'll find them.' Clive chauffeured me along the track, and we headed towards the main gate, a kilometre away. There were the boys, right by the gate. Worry tumbled with guilty emotions: were they there trying to tell us they wanted to go, or were they trying to get back in the last paddock they were in? There was so much grass around; why did they feel the need to walk along this track? Perhaps they were searching for more water? Remorse overwhelmed me all over again.

As I hopped off the cart and walked towards them, as a group they strode straight to me, heads down, ears up, clearly pleased to see me. I'd just dumped them off and not given them a second thought; they were as confused as I, and I hadn't taken that into account!

Noel and Andrea had caught us up, and we led them back to the horse paddock, back to Jet and Cedar. The boys supped from the trough and wandered off as if nothing had happened. Jet and Cedar and their old paddock meant home to them.

'Please join us tomorrow for Christmas lunch; we have a few people coming,' said Andrea.

'I can't contribute, unless you want noodles?' I smiled tiredly.

'Don't be ridiculous – you need feeding up. Just bring yourselves and some good yarns.'

I could do nothing but hug her.

Then the tears started again as I walked back into our old cottage. It was gleaming: a beautiful Christmas tree adorned with pretty decorations stood in the lounge, gifts neatly lay around the stem, wine in the fridge with bread, milk, tea, coffee, and homemade cake and cookies. It was tremendous. Clive and Andrea run a six-hundred acre farm together, Andrea works two other jobs, they keep an enormous vegetable garden going, and they do not have one moment of spare time. Yet, they made time for us.

The soft chairs with arm-rests and back support made Noel and I groan in pleasure. We hugged each other often, reassured, smiled, and cried. The hot shower nearly expired with overuse. It was better than five-star luxury.

Christmas was filled with good cheer and lovely friends, but decisions would have to be made soon. I finished the journey as I started – with injuries – but we'd all changed. We changed those boys' lives. Like a bullied person gaining the confidence to speak out, allowing him to be himself completely, they'd realised that they had something to offer. They were proud, fit, confident, and unswervingly loyal.

Of course, Noel and I changed, but it wasn't the journey that changed us the most – it was those boys. What we had done for them, they had given us back in spades. They are forever deeply folded within our hearts. We relied on them, and they knew it, so they gave. They gave us their all, they gave us their trust, they put their fear in our hands, they offered us their love and cheeky antics. But so much more than that, they gave us – unwaveringly, utterly, and without question - their hearts.

Epilogue

Horses love you back. I've always known this, but now I've witnessed and been part of a bond that, at times, overwhelmed me. Living with horses day and night is very different from a day-to-day relationship. What's more, it surprised Noel. His comments of, 'we have to remember they are just horses,' are long gone – replaced with tears of longing to be back with our family.

I've learned that with patience and kindness anything is possible. People doubted our sanity when we gave homes to trotters, some of which had not been ridden. While Noel and I didn't fare well on the journey, those boys were nothing short of magnificent.

I know my body doesn't need meat that often (but I do crave it, and indulge from time to time), and bruises are so much more painful in your forties!

I tasted failure, and my heart has broken all over again with saying farewell to my beautiful boys, but it's making me stronger – most days. I know I'll rescue more horses and I'll love them, and my heart will break all over again when I find them their forever homes. I'll remind myself that I will be breaking my own heart with my decisions; no one else will be doing it – these will be my choices.

I've learned you don't need much. And that until I have travelled someone else's journey I cannot know how tough or complex it is.

I know how much I love Noel and he loves me; that never altered – never will.

I've *really* learned how to swear: they say sailors swear – but I don't think I've stopped since that trip!

I now know how tough cowboys are.

I've learned to yell!

And I've learned, that yes, it was *enough* to experience what we had – it was plenty... for now.

Anywhere, at any time, we are all only just clinging to the thread of life – the unexpected could be tomorrow, tonight, next week. There's not enough time to ponder or procrastinate.

I still think about my mortality too and deny it at the same time. The end of this journey was another beginning. I have more purpose and motivation to live on my terms. Time gushes past relentlessly, and it will run out. I have many lives to save before then, and for the first time I can clearly see the future. I see a large green meadow dotted with horses who just need a chance.

Anne

We are still great friends with Anne. We miss her terribly. While I was writing this book, Anne's memory was greater than mine, so we conversed about times, distances, and events. Here's a quote from a recent email:

'It was such a lovely adventure for me watching you and Noel do all the hard yakka while I drove home to a comfy bed, with my dogs who didn't need to be groomed, pedicured, and saddled up every day.'

We love you Anne!

Sue

As I write Sue is traversing the track with only the company of her trusty steed Bob! She started with a friend who had to stop for injury reasons. She then paired up with another lady, who also had to stop when her horses suffered injuries. She's not always alone though; Bill has been a marvellous back-up in the truck. What an amazing lady. There are days Bill can't reach her, so Sue and Bob meander alone. I am utterly jealous! My hat goes off to you Sue!

Clive and Andrea

Still great friends, and they continue to support us in whatever mad-cap adventure we take on. They are wonderful people.

The boys - where are they now?

The boys are with friends while we spend time nearer my family in the northern hemisphere. I think about them every day. They are as healthy as they've ever been; 'they're so shiny you can see your reflection in their coats,' we're told, and we have the pictures to prove it.

Our only regret is splitting the team, but they all have new buddies, are cared for and loved, and just the tiniest bit spoiled – well, okay, quite a bit!

Stevie and Spirit are together, making new friends and taking on more trails, for just a day or two at a time. They no longer show their ribs, and they look happy and bright-eyed.

Charlie, Ned, and Dom are together in paradise: groomed every day, occasionally ridden, and treated royally. Ned and Charlie have fondly earned the term 'the villains,' as Charlie is the boss, and Ned feels it is still necessary to keep Dom in check. Dom, the baby, just loves people and his two mates and is 'the biggest sook.'

We receive regular pictures and up-dates; I smile and cry every time.

And us

If you want to travel by horse, without support, you have to be happy with going back in time – to over a hundred years ago. Grovelling around in the dirt is part of life while everyone else has moved on, stepping out of cars immaculately dressed.

We're still not immaculately dressed: how can you be while renovating a 1920s Dutch barge in France during winter? But that's another story.

List of gear

Two large canvas bags (usually on Ned)

Four rectangular-shaped buckets in each canvas bag (each held ten litres of water)

Feed for horses – usually only five kilograms maximum

Nose bags for feed

Hobbles

Twenty plastic electric fence poles

Fifty metres of electric fence on a make-shift winder

2 x D batteries for the electric fence (and two spares)

Electric fence energiser

Rope halters with reins, instead of bridles (and spares)

3 x Pack-saddles (2 x purpose made pack-saddles, 1 x riding saddle with adjustments to carry packs)

2 x Regular saddles

Saddle blankets (We started with incredibly thick, large blankets for the pack-saddles; however, they were heavy, and we opted for thinner, lighter blankets.)

Packing bags – started with four large plastic panniers, switched to eight backpacks

Saddle-bags – behind the two riding saddles ("hand bags!")

Horses' boots – sometimes carried, sometimes worn.

Hoof picks

Mozzie nets for us and horses

Rugs for each horse

Two soft brushes (from house hold dustpan/brush set) – with handles cut off

First aid kits (one each in case we became separated)

First aid kit for horses

Clothes – I had two t-shirts, a shirt, two pairs of pants, underwear, long-johns, two jumpers, socks and wet weather gear. Noel had the same but more cotton shirts instead of t-shirts.

Boots and thongs (flip-flops)

Tent – Later we had two tents (plus a tent tarp that went over the two tents and tent poles).

Sleeping bags (goose down) and inner-sheet

Down-filled mattresses (blow-up)

Blow-up pillow

Food – Noodles, packet soups, Snickers bars, porridge, Vegemite, oil, oats, granola bars, some small fruit and vegetables, small packets of sauces, a few dried-meals, pasta, salami, cheese, chocolate, nuts, dried fruit, sweet chilli sauce, rice, peanut butter, crackers, dried potato, dried peas

Water bottles

Wash gear – small bottle of shampoo, cake of soap

Comb – although I rarely brushed my hair. A finger-comb worked well.

Plastic knife, fork and spoon each

Plastic bowl each

Cup each

Toilet rolls

Absorbent towel each for Noel and me and one for the horses

Sun hats

Nail clippers

Scissors

Small mirror

Small radio each

Book each (I was reading a Dick Francis novel; I love his style and characters. I am a big fan. Noel enjoys Mr Francis, too, and would have read the same book. Noel chose thrillers; anything that had nothing to do with the trail!)

Moisturising cream

Sun cream

Razor blades

Scales for weighing gear
Tea-cloth
Torches and matches
Washing-up liquid
Tea-towel
2 billies (pots), one for water, one for cooking (We gave away the frying pan.)
Small-hand (folding) shovel
Sharp knife each
Pain-killers, lots of pain-killers!
Spare rope
Riding hats and sun hats/caps
Glasses (prescription and sun-glasses)
Small solar cell for charging batteries (radio) and phones
Mobile phone
Claw hammer (with claw cut off!)
Notebook and pen
Bank card/cash
Horse documents (inoculation information/vet check/dentist check details/dates)
Sewing gear, repair kit
Leatherman – tools/knives in pouch
Trail maps and guides – to help lighten our load we carried the relevant sections only, and arranged the following sections to be mailed to us at appropriate opportunities.
Waterproof map holder (slung off saddle pommel)
Hair ties (to keep my unruly mop out of the way)
Rasp for horses' feet
Farrier's knife/hoof-pick
Lip balm
2 x lightweight fold up water bags (brilliant) with straps and string to tie up in a tree

20m x 6mm nylon rope
Mane combs
Horse fly nets
Machete
Walkie-talkies (never used)
GPS (Global Positioning System)
We started with stools (small fold-up) but discarded these at Crookwell, together with the farrier's apron, whips, and additional clothing and spares.

Glossary

ACT - Australian Capital Territory is a territory in southeast Australia, enclaved within New South Wales.

Beanies – Woolly hats

Billabong – A branch of a river forming a backwater or stagnant pool, made by water flowing from the main stream during a flood

BNT – Bicentennial National Trail. Australia's long distance, multi-use recreational trekking route, stretching 5,330 kilometres from Cooktown in Queensland to Healesville in Victoria.

Cavalletti – These are small jumps: a thin pole connected to two crosses for horses to jump over. The name cavalletti is used by the Bicentennial National Trail and National Parks for the poles we had to traverse along the trail. Some people also refer to them as 'poles.'

Fetlock joint – Similar to an ankle

hh (as in 16hh) – An abbreviation for hands high. The measure of a hand is four inches. Proper denotation of a horse's height is with the number of whole hands followed by the number of parts of a hand or inches remaining. A 16-hand horse would be written 16hh or 16.0hh.

Hobbles – Devices for tying or strapping together the legs of a horse (or other animal) to prevent it from straying (we used canvas strapping). To hobble a horse is to restrict its movements, so he/she can only take very small steps.

Leg-aids – The leg aids are one of the most basic and 'natural' aids we have to communicate with the horse. All riders regularly use their legs to give messages to the horse, but most of the time, the legs mean go faster or change gait.

NSW – New South Wales, a state in Australia

Sound – No lameness

SPPHA – Standardbred Pleasure and Performance Horse Association (of NSW). The SPPHA is a not-for-profit association, founded in 1993 to promote Standardbred horses in their lives after racing.

Standardbred – The Standardbred is bred for harness racing. The breed ranges in height from 14hh to 17+hh, and body type can vary from stocky to refined.

Strangles – Also known as equine distemper, strangles is a contagious upper respiratory tract infection in horses and other equines caused by a bacterium, *Streptococcus*.

Tetanus – Tetanus is a dangerous nerve ailment caused by the toxin of a common bacterium, *Clostridium tetani*. Bacterial spores are found in soil, where they can remain infectious for more than forty years. If the spores enter a wound that penetrates the skin and extends deeper than oxygen can reach, they germinate and produce a toxin that enters the bloodstream.

Travellers – Ready-made travel 'bandages' or 'boots' that are simply fastened with Velcro around the horses' bottom legs to protect them while in a trailer/float or horse truck.

TSR – Travelling Stock Reserves are fenced paddocks set aside at strategic distances to allow overnight watering and camping of stock.

From the Author

Thanks for purchasing and reading *A Standard Journey* – I hope you enjoyed it.

A lot of people don't realise that the best way to help an author is to leave a review. So, if you did enjoy my story, please return to the site you purchased it from and say a few words. It doesn't need to be long: just saying what you thought is fine, and so very much appreciated.

I love hearing from readers and authors alike, so if you'd like to stay in touch and be the first to know about forthcoming books and/or follow our escapades, why not drop by and visit us at:

www.jackieparry.com
www.noelandjackiesjourneys.com
FB: Noel and Jackie's Journeys
Twitter: NandJJourneys

If you enjoy memoirs take a look at We Love Memoirs on Facebook.

Acknowledgements

A huge thank you to the following people for their feedback and support during the writing process for *A Standard Journey*: Rachel Amphlett, Rochelle Carlton, Carole & Barrie Erdman Grant, Tracy Slater, Anne Norris, Shelley Wright, Nick Furmidge, and Andrea Stafford.

My deepest gratitude and respect goes to my editors Danielle Rose and Tara Gilboy at Narrative Ink Editing LLC. Not only did they help me shape my story to what it should be but they helped take it to another level. They also mentored, taught, suggested, reassured, and challenged me to stretch my thoughts and skills.

Noel and I send our thanks also to the SPPHA for the incredible and relentless job they do.

To the people who manage the BNT too, we share our thanks. While it is not perfect, it is quite splendid in places, and what a feat to have a trail of that magnitude open to everyone. We hope you continue your wonderful work.

A huge thank you to the BNT co-ordinators that helped us voluntarily – you were wonderful, and we appreciated everything you did for us.

Thanks go to Web Diversion Designs for another great cover.

To my family and friends – thanks for all your support in whatever form you've provided it. I love writing and appreciate everyone allowing me the time I need to do so.

To everyone who's left reviews and connects via social media, I sincerely thank you too. Your positive messages and marvellous reviews mean more to me than you'll ever know.

Available in paperback, ebook, or audio on Amazon
Of Foreign Build ISBN: 978-0-9875515-4-2
Amazon link: http://geni.us/ipq

Reviews:

"This is a literary masterpiece."

"This book reads like a mystery novel."

"I couldn't wait for the next chapter."

Available in paperback or ebook on Amazon
Cruisers' AA ISBN: 978-0-9875515-0-4
Amazon link: http://geni.us/3sKJ

Reviews:

"…probably the most comprehensive reference book designed for preparation for a cruising life."

"… a remarkable reference [book]. … There is a depth of information that beggars the imagination."

"This is a new & fascinating insight on how to go cruising."

2 hemispheres, 2 people, and 1 boat

This Is It

Jackie Parry

Available in paperback or ebook on Amazon
This Is It ISBN: 978-0-9875515-8-0
Amazon link: http://goo.gl/bqIZTV

Reviews:
"It made me laugh out loud, it also made me cry; it had me perching on the edge of my seat."
"This story is raw, emotional, and dangerous!"
"I couldn't put it down!"

Excerpt from This Is It – 2 hemispheres, 2 people, and 1 boat

1
_____

Will it be Enough?

'I think it's what we should do.'

Leaning on the sink, I stared out the kitchen window. The sulphur-crested cockatoos broke the silence with an ear-piercing squawk.

'While we're young and fit enough,' Noel continued.

Rainbow lorikeets flitted between the plump maple trees that were dominating the postage-stamp garden behind our cottage in Greenwell Point, New South Wales.

Was I ready to leave all this again?

Could I pack up our life's possessions and leave the stability of owning a house and living in a small community?

We'd done it before, but I was in my twenties then.

Would it be vastly different in my forties?

Was Noel right? After all, what is life for if you're not wringing out every last drop?

'Come and have a look at this boat – it'd suit us.'

Twisting from the stainless basin, I peered into the interior gloom and waited for my eyes to adjust. I raised my eyebrows at my grinning husband who sat with confidence by the computer; he knew I'd agree. I wasn't going to say no to a new escapade; but another sailing adventure? I'd had my heart set on exploring Europe by barge.

Walking towards my buddy and his aura of excitement, I rolled my eyes. Convincing me was easy, and the flutter of anticipation stirred my stomach.

'Will it be enough?' I asked, thinking of all the sailing miles already under our belts.

'Enough? Enough! You don't think buying a boat in a foreign country, preparing it to cross oceans, *and* sailing back to Australia is enough?'

'That's not what I meant.'

'What do you mean, then? You know it's not an easy task.'

I wasn't sure what I was trying to say. Perhaps it was because we'd already sailed around the globe on *Mariah*, a thirty-three foot boat. I'm not saying it was easy or that I felt as though we'd *been there, done that*. I simply hadn't thought deeply enough about this new idea. I was thinking about an old steel barge on the European canals, which would be easier, but it was a different challenge – something new.

I constantly crave that kick-in-the-gut emotion from the delicious mix of fear and thrill that a new challenge offers. I must put myself out there and have a plan in motion that makes my heart jump. I need to push myself to new levels, fill my core with wonder, gasp with joy, and quake with fear!

Would another sailing trip do this? Later, this thought would come-back and slap me hard on the face.

My jumbled emotions and thoughts made little sense to me, but that was nothing new.

How challenging would a barge be? That was the second thought that'd turn around and laugh in my face much later on.

I questioned my ability to sit through night watches, though. I need eight hours of solid sleep. How would I cope with four to six hour shifts while crossing an ocean now that I was staring at my forties?

'Buck up,' I muttered to myself. 'You're not too old yet!'

But these thoughts carried me off and caused a certain amount of angst that swirled with the anticipation of sailing again.

Noel and I worked for a couple of years, squirreled away our earnings, and dashed off on another voyage – not a few weeks in a foreign land, but a living exploit. We weren't rich, just careful with our money. We had no debts; we never bought something unless it was imperative – whether it was for the house, for us, or the escapade.

Fashion wasn't important, nor was the latest phone or computer. If our gear worked fine, that was enough.

We didn't use credit cards. We steered clear of unnecessary constraints like careers and mortgages. Our life was the journey – the adventure – we spent more nomadic-time than working-for-someone-else time, and that balance was shifting even further in our wandering favour.

The buying-a-boat-in-America idea grew from living in the USA for a year (on *Mariah*, while traversing The Great Loop). We had found that boat prices in the States were less expensive than in Australia. We circumnavigated on our first boat, *Mariah*, ultimately sailing into Greenwell Point NSW, the closest safe harbour to family – and where the next escapade was taking shape.

'If we found a boat cheap enough, used our skills to transform it into a good sea-going vessel and comfortable home, when we've finished our trip, the boat sale may end up funding the entire trip.'

'You mean it pays for itself?' I asked.

'Yes, and our living on board expenses for a few years. That's pretty much what happened with *Mariah*.'

Making money on boats was not easy; it was rare to sell for a profit.

Discussions on this scheme rolled in and out of our lives like a tide across a sandy beach; at times, the tide was out and a damp beach allowed only a trickle of thoughts to seep in; other times, our ideas raged upon a flood tide with plans that rolled and bobbed on the surface.

* * *

Over the following year, while we worked at our maritime teaching jobs at Technical and Further Education (TAFE), I became an Internet widow while Noel scoured the USA for our next boat. The idea settled in my muddled mind, and I started to grasp the enormity of the undertaking.

The momentum gathered me up and swept us both along. Enthusiastically, I immersed myself in the hectic but exhilarating project of leaving Australia, renting out our home, resigning from our jobs, liberating ourselves from our possessions, and bidding farewell to family and friends once again.

With intrepid excitement and a smidgen of horror—*what on earth are we doing?* – we landed in San Francisco, hauling just the clothes on our backs and one small bag each. Our bags bulged out at awkward boat equipment angles; they acquired some odd looks. Not so apparent to our fellow passengers was the huge dollop of determination that sat squarely on our shoulders.

* * *

The idea of buying a boat in the States was also a good excuse to explore the bejewelled Pacific Ocean once again. On our last boat, we discovered a smattering of her diamonds. This time, we weren't interested in traversing the Panama Canal a second time, and we'd already sailed much of the east coast and the inland waterways of

254

America, including the Great Lakes, the Ohio River, and the Mississippi River.

Exploring new parts of the vast ocean was top of the list.

Noel and I grew up with British history. Bligh held particular interest, because he became Australia's Governor fifteen years after the mutiny in 1789. Noel chomped through many historical books detailing HMS Bounty, the maligned Bligh, and the mutiny. I devoured Hollywood's interpretations through Mel Gibson, Marlon Brando, Clark Gable (as Fletcher Christian), and Anthony Hopkins (playing Bligh in The Bounty).

Sailing from America towards Australia afforded us the opportunity to sail down to Pitcairn's latitude, en route sat Easter Island, the remotest inhabited island in the world. If you have sailed to one, why not visit the other?

Although, the more recent Pitcairn history supervised a portion of my mind.

Surely that black cloud has long gone.

On the lighter side, extraordinary viewpoints encouraged our aspirations.

As friends and relations caught wind of our plans and the whispers fanned out, sailing 'experts' and travelling 'specialists' declared our strategy too hard.

'They can't do that!'

'You can't anchor there!'

'It's too far!'

Self-professed authorities didn't quell our thirst for this demanding voyage. We'd dealt with nay-sayers all our travelling lives. Every time we would prove them wrong, and each negative comment stimulated our gypsy spirit with the motivation to accomplish.

It emerged that Noel's main goal was to sail to the remotest inhabited island in the world: Easter Island. I was wrapped up in that dream, so it became mine, too – but, fundamentally, my role was to support Noel in his endeavours and help make it happen. That may be why I was wondering if this was enough.

I craved the freedom of sailing and travelling with our home; home being where we belonged, a refuge from the outside world, a safe haven of comparative peace, and the ability to travel with our own bed, pillow, and favourite drinking mug. The fact that a home can, strangely enough, be a bobbing cork in the shape of a cruising boat is a remarkable concurrence.

The idea embodied our souls; it came alive, evolved, carrying us along as if it was the director and we were just the puppets. The animated scheme developed into a good excuse to return to our voyaging lives, because that was when we had a distinct purpose; besides, we were good at it. *Would we be this time, though? Or had the sailing community been on the money? Did our dreams outstretch our ability?*

Futher reading, reviews, and purchase on Amazon.

Lightning Source UK Ltd.
Milton Keynes UK
UKHW021139191218
334269UK00008B/139/P

9 780987 551566